"The first motion you make to do that, I'll shoot you dead!"

LOW TWELVE

"BY THEIR DEEDS YE SHALL KNOW THEM"

A Series of Striking and Truthful Incidents illustrative of the fidelity of Free Masons to one another in times of distress and danger

By

EDWARD S. ELLIS, A.M.

P. M. Trenton (N. J.) Lodge, No. 5
F. & A. M.

Stone Guild Publishing
Plano, Texas
http://www.stoneguildpublishing.com/

2009

Originally Published By:
F. R. NIGLUTSCH
1907

This Edition Copyright © 2008
Stone Guild Publishing, Inc.
Plano, Texas
http://www.stoneguildpublishing.com/

First Paperback Edition 2009

ISBN-13 978-1-60532-048-9
ISBN-10 1-60532-048-X

10 9 8 7 6 5 4 3 2

INTRODUCTION

IT is to be feared that some enthusiastic writers on Free Masonry give the order an antiquity that is more or less imaginative. One especially ardent author makes the patriarch's archs and other noted Biblical characters Free Masons, and insists that several of the Saviour's disciples were members of the order. Free Masonry, nonetheless, is the oldest existing organization of a charitable nature in the history of mankind.

During the middle Ages, the Mason brotherhoods were organized corporations, resembling in a general way the other guilds, with rules of their own, and recruited from a body of apprentices who had served a period of probation. The time referred to was a church-building age, and men skilled in the hewing and setting of stones were in demand and held in high esteem. When a great church or cathedral was to be built, skillful masons gathered from distant quarters to assist those of the neighborhood in the work. A master was chosen, who superintended the whole, and every tenth man was a warden with authority over the rest.

It followed, therefore, that a mason, after serving his apprenticeship, could not settle down, like other craftsmen, among his neighbors, but was obliged to travel in order to find employment. It was advisable that all members of the fraternity should possess the means of making themselves known to one another and thus avoid the necessity of proving their skill as craftsmen. In order to do so, and to enable a mason to claim the hospitality of his brother masons, a system of symbols was devised, in which every mason was initiated and which he was pledged to keep secret.

The term "Free," as applied to the craft, arose from the fact that its members were exempted by several papal bulls from the laws, which governed ordinary laborers, as well as from the various burdens imposed upon the working classes in England and on the Continent. These laws bound the Free Masons to certain religious duties, and it was natural that a craft whose principal business was church building should receive the special attention and care of the clergy. So marked became the influence of the Free Masons that the jealousy of the Church was aroused long before the Reformation. Henry of Beaufort, Cardinal of Winchester, instigated the passage of an act, during the minority of Henry VI., which forbade the Masons to hold their accustomed chapters and assemblies. However, the act was never enforced, and when Henry VI. became of age he joined the order, while Henry VII. was the Grand Master in England.

The origin of operative masonry is traced back by many to the old Roman Empire, the Pharaohs, and the Temple of Solomon, even to the Tower of Babel and to the Ark of Noah. Speculative Free Masonry originated in England and dates from the seventeenth century. Its foundation lies in the "practice of moral and social virtue," its characteristic feature being charity in the broadest sense, brotherly love, relief and truth. It is because of this foundation, so closely approaching that which is divine, that the growth, prosperity and permanence of the noble institution are due. It has withstood every shock and will continue its beneficent sway to the end of time.

Charles II. and William III. were Masons, and a seeming connection with operative masonry was kept up by the appointment of Sir Christopher Wren to the office of Grand Master. The Scottish lodges claim origin among the foreign masons who came to Scotland in 1150 to build Kilwinning Abbey; those of England go back to an assemblage of masons held by St. Alban at York in 926. The mother lodges of York and Kilwinning were, with a few slight exceptions, the parents of all the lodges that were formed in different parts of Great Britain. The admirable character of the order was attested in 1799, when in the act passed in England for the suppression of secret societies, Free Masonry was the only one excepted from the operation of the law. A Grand Lodge was formed in London in 1717, with power to grant charters to other lodges, and the constitutions of the fraternity were first published under its sanction. From this fountain Free Masonry has spread to every quarter of the globe.

Now and then, we Masons are amused by statements concerning female members of our order. Some years ago, it was claimed by a number of newspapers that a certain famous woman sculptor of Washington was a Free Mason. The writer of this asked for the name of the lodge in which she was initiated and a few other particulars. The reply was given that she was a member of one of the lodges instituted by the then Empress Eugenie of France. My next audacious question was as to where the Empress got her authority for chartering Masonic lodges. The intimation was further made that she was no more a Free Mason than the gilt figurehead of a man-of-war. Every real Mason knows that there never was, is not and never will or can be a female Free Mason. Let our sisters remain content with the reply of a gallant brother:

"You were *born* Masons; any initiation or ceremony would be superfluous; therefore, we do not insult you by any such proposition."

Nonetheless, there is respectable authority for believing that three women have taken the first step in Masonry. It is said that Mrs. Beaton, of Norfolk, England, learned the secrets of the Entered Apprentice degree by hiding herself in the wainscoting of a lodge room. She lived well beyond four-score, and, incredible as it may sound, kept her secret inviolate. Madame de Xaintrailles, it is claimed, was initiated in the first degree by the Freres-Artistes lodge, in Paris, more than a hundred years ago, and the Hon. Mrs. Aldworth was similarly honored. The most that can be said, therefore, is that these women knew simply the first step of Freemasonry.*

It was inevitable that the order should suffer persecution at the hands of degenerates and those who were ignorant of its real spirit. The most noted example of late years was Gabriel Jogand-Pages, a Frenchman born in 1854. His publications against Free Masonry were grotesquely monstrous, but for a time gained many believers. The fact that they were denied by such distinguished Free Masons as Emperor William I., Bismarck and the Prince of Wales added to the excitement caused by the book, of which hundreds of thousands of copies

---

*A venerable Free Mason once told me that many years ago, he met a very old brother who said he was present on one of the memorable occasions when it is claimed that a woman was made an Entered Apprentice Mason. The oath, which she was compelled to take, far from being the legitimate one of that degree, was simply a solemn pledge, under the most fearful penalties, never to reveal any of the secrets, which she had discovered. I cannot help suspecting that in all the instances of these alleged initiations, a similar course was followed, and that no woman was ever made so much as a real Entered Apprentice. Doubtless, the awfulness of the oath and penalty had much to do in keeping her lips sealed regarding the little she had learned. No Free Mason needs to be reminded that it is simply *impossible* for any woman to become a member of our order.

were sold. In 1897, Jogand-Pages publicly confessed that everything written by him against the order was an intentional lie.

The greatest blow ever received by Free Masonry in this country was in 1826, and it did not recover therefrom for twenty years. The particulars of this affair are given in the succeeding pages. From that time, the opposition to the order rapidly declined, finally to disappear altogether. To-day, with nearly a million of members in the United States, it is stronger than ever and steadily growing. Bishop Henry C. Potter said in 1901:

"Free Masonry, however, is in my view of it a great deal more than a mutual benefit association. In one sense, wild and extravagant as the words may sound, it is the most remarkable and altogether unique institution on earth. Will you tell me of any other that girdles the world with its fellowship and gathers all races and the most ancient religions, as well as our own, into its brotherhood? Will you tell me of any other that is as old or older; more brilliant in its history; more honored in its constituency, and more picturesque in its traditions? To-day it lies in the hand of the modern man largely an unused tool, capable of great achievements for God, for country, for mankind, but doing very little. For one, I believe that circumstances may easily arise when the highest and most sacred of all freedoms being threatened in this land, Free Masonry may be its most powerful defender, unifying all minds and commanding our best citizenship."

Let it be understood that we are not trying to apologize or make any plea for Free Masonry. No member is permitted to ask any outsider to join the order and no man can be admitted if in a secret ballot a single vote appears against him. In order to show the beneficent character of the order, the following landmarks or unchangeable laws are quoted from the list given by Dr. Mackey:

"Every candidate for initiation must be a man, free born and of lawful age; he must believe in the existence of God as the Great Architect of the universe; he must believe in a resurrection to a future life; a book of the law of God must constitute an indispensable part of the furniture of every lodge; all men in the sight of God are equal, and meet in the lodge on one common level."

The universality of the order was set forth by Charles Whitlock Moore, of Massachusetts, in 1856, at the centennial anniversary of St. Andrew's Lodge, Boston:

"At the reorganization of the craft and the establishment of the present Grand Lodge of England, in 1717, we laid aside our operative character, and with it all pretensions to extraordinary skill in architectural science. We then became a purely moral and benevolent association, whose great aim is the development and cultivation of the moral sentiment, the social principle, and the benevolent affections, a higher reverence for God, and a warmer love for man. New laws and regulations, adapted to the changed condition of the institution, were then made, an entire revolution in its governmental policy took place, order and system obtained where neither had previously existed, and England became the great central point of Masonry for the whole world.

"From this source have lodges, grand and subordinate, at various times been established, and still exist and flourish in France and Switzerland; in all the German states save Austria (and there at different times and for short seasons); all up and down the classic shores of the Rhine; in Prussia; Holland, Belgium, Saxony, Hanover, Sweden, Denmark, Russia and even in fallen Poland; in Italy and Spain (under cover of secrecy); in various parts of Asia; in Turkey; in

Syria (as at Aleppo, where an English lodge was established more than a century ago); in all the East India settlements, in Bengal, Bombay, Madras (in all of which lodges are numerous); in China, where there is a Provincial Grand Master and several lodges; in various parts of Africa, as at the Cape of Good Hope and at Sierra Leone; on the Gambia and on the Nile; in all the larger islands of the Pacific and Indian oceans, as at Ceylon, Sumatra, St. Helena, Mauritius, Madagascar; the Sandwich group; in all the principal settlements of Australia, as at Adelaide, Melbourne, Parramatta, Sidney, New Zealand; in Greece, where there is a grand lodge; in Algeria, in Tunis, in the empire of Morocco, and wherever else in the Old World the genius of civilization has obtained a standpoint, or Christianity has erected the banner of the Cross.

"In all the West India Islands and in various parts of South America, as in Peru, Venezuela, New Granada, Guiana, Brazil, Chile, etc., Masonry is prospering as never before.... In Mexico, even, respectable lodges are maintained, despite the opposition of a bigoted priesthood; and in all British America, from Newfoundland, through Nova Scotia and the Canadas to the icy regions of the North, Masonic lodges and Masonic brethren may be found, 'to feed the hungry, clothe the naked and bind up the wounds of the afflicted.'"

Ancient Free Masonry consists of the three degrees—Entered Apprentice, Fellow Craft and Master Mason. Upon these are based the York rite and the Scottish rite. The former takes its name from the city of York, in the north of England, where the annual and general assemblies of the craft were re-established in A.D. 926. In addition to the symbolic degrees, it includes Capitular, Cryptic and Chivalric grades, conferred in bodies known respectively as the Chapter,

Council and Commandery. The Chapter has four degrees — Mark Master, Past Master, Most Excellent Master and the Royal Arch, together with an honorary order of high priesthood. The Council has two degrees—Royal Master and Select Master. The Commandery has three orders—Knight of the Red Cross, Knight Templar and Knight of Malta.

Free Masonry has been tardy in admitting the African race to recognition. The first Negroes made Freemasons were Prince Hall and fourteen colored citizens of Boston. The travelling lodge of a British regiment in 1775 conferred the symbolic degrees upon them. England granted them a charter in 1787, and the first Masonic lodge, with Prince Hall as Master, was instituted. In 1797 a second Negro lodge was established in Philadelphia and a third soon after in Providence. These three lodges united in forming a grand lodge in 1808, which in 1827 declared itself independent of England. Our colored grand lodges now number over thirty. The legality of these Masons is indisputable, but as much can hardly be said of the Negro Royal Arch Masons, Commandery and Scottish rite. Liberia, on the west coast of Africa, has had a legitimate grand lodge for sixty years. In some parts of Germany Jews are not admitted as candidates, nor are they recognized as such individually. These isolated instances of race prejudice must disappear with the progress of enlightenment and real brotherhood.

It has seemed to me and many of the brethren that a collection of incidents illustrative of the true nature of Freemasonry will be interesting and instructive. I find these incidents so numerous that a selection is difficult. I have been careful to give only those that in my judgment are authentic. Truth compels me to admit, however, that the principal sketch, which follows, although founded upon fact

(I was present in the lodge when Jared J. Jennings made his entrance as described, and he told me he was made a Mason among the Chippewa Indians), contains some imaginative touches, which I am sure will not be found inconsistent with the real spirit of Freemasonry.

    I am prompted to add for the benefit of my brethren that as a Masonic authority, Robert Freke Gould's "Unabridged History of Freemasonry throughout the World" stands without a peer or rival. It has received the highest encomiums from the foremost Freemasons, living and dead, and is a mine of invaluable information to the members of the Order everywhere.

E. S. E.

UPPER MONCLAIR, N. J., 1908.

CONTENTS

I.	Low Twelve	17
II.	" "	29
III.	" "	40
IV.	" "	50
V.	" "	62
VI.	" "	73
VII.	After Ten Years	86
VIII.	Camping on His Trail	104
IX.	A Typical Lodge	119
X.	Tried by Fire	133
XI.	A Lively Time	148
XII.	The Man Who Saved President Diaz	167
XIII.	On the Summit of the Rocky Mountains—First Masonic Lodge Held in Montana	176
XIV.	True to His Oath—A Legend of the New Jersey Coast	180
XV.	A Soldier of Fortune	190
XVI.	My Ghost	196
XVII.	Reminiscences	209
XVIII.	"For God's Sake, 'Lige, Flee to theMountains!"	219
XIX.	The Abduction of William Morgan	234
XX.	Masonic Grand Lodges in the United States and British America	248

LIST OF ILLUSTRATIONS

"The first motion you make to do that, I'll shoot you dead!"	*Frontispiece*
"Don't trust *any* of your Indian scouts"	27
"It was Geronimo himself"	51
"It was a night of tragedy"	79
"I should like to know what *that* means!"	99
The President's Rebuke	121
"You had better adjourn your lodge at once and send the brethren home"	128
Ben McCulloch, the Texan Ranger, and Bishop Janes, of the M. E. Church	139
"Yank, do you see that piece of woods?"	145
In dire extremity	155
A bad fix for President Diaz	171
"You must not try to go home to-night"	183
"I aimed straight at him and let fly"	203
Reminiscences	211
"Ride, Larry, ride, for a life is at stake!"	229
The Traitor	245

LOW TWELVE

I

I SHALL never forget the visitor that we had at our lodge one evening in the early winter of 1885. I should state that my name is Alfred B. Chichester, that at that time I was a lieutenant of cavalry, stationed in the Southwest, and after two years' arduous service was visiting my home in the East on furlough. Having been a Mason only a brief while, I never failed to attend the regular and generally the special meetings of the lodge. Sometimes we become neglectful as we grow older in the order, but the flush of a new and beautiful experience gave a peculiar zest to the visits on my part.

We were on the third degree when a card was sent in by the Tyler announcing that Jared J. Jennings, claiming to be a Master Mason, asked for a seat among his brethren. Perhaps I was more alert than the others were, for in listening to the announcement I noticed that the officer did not name the lodge from which the stranger hailed. The Master failed to observe the omission, and appointed the usual committee to go outside and examine the applicant. I was not a member of the committee, which returned some time later with the information that they had examined the brother and found him to be a bright Mason. Again, while giving his name, they omitted that of his lodge. The Master ordered his admission, and a minute afterward, he entered.

Every one in the lodge was struck by his appearance. I remember the thought at once occurred to me that he was the picture of William Penn, the Quaker founder of Philadelphia, and Proprietor of the State named in his honor. He was dressed in the attire of the Friends, had a handsome, smoothly shaven face, with long auburn hair curling about his shoulders, and was slightly inclined to corpulency. His yellow waistcoat with its flapping pockets descended low in front, his brown coat had similar huge flaps, but the trousers were of modern cut. Unlike Father Penn, however, he wore a massive gold chain, to which a handsome Masonic medal was pendent, and a fine diamond sparkled on his ruffled shirtfront. Evidently, he was a man of comfortable means.

His behavior after entering the lodge was as remarkable as his appearance. When facing the East he did not once look up, but stood with his eyes fixed on the floor at his feet. Then he began walking slowly forward, still gazing downward. Every one curiously watched him, wondering what he meant.

Suddenly, when he had reached a certain point, he stopped with an expression as of fear on his face, threw up his hands, and leaped backward a couple of paces, for all the world like a person who hears the warning whirr of a rattlesnake in the path in front of him. However, it was observable that in making this singular movement, he did precisely what he should have done with his hands. He was "all right."

The Master invited him to a seat among the brethren, and courteously thanking him with an inclination of the head, Brother Jennings looked around, and seeing a vacant place at my side bowed to me with a pleasing smile and sat down.

There was something attractive to me in all this, as well as in the singular appearance of the man, and I reached out my hand. He shook it warmly, crossed his shapely legs, folded his arms and fixed his attention upon the Master. Some time later, the lodge was called to refreshment and officers and brethren mingled on the floor. I may add at this point for the benefit of those who are not Masons, that "refreshment" in a lodge means a time when all business is suspended, generally while candidates are being prepared in the anteroom for some degree. It corresponds to recess in school, and does not imply that anything in the nature of feasting or eating is going on.

The occasion gave a chance for the Master, wardens and such brothers as chose to gather around the stranger and chat with him. I was in the little knot. The Master was the first to speak.

"Brother Jennings, what lodge do you hail from?"

He smiled significantly.

"Don't feel apprehensive when I tell you that my lodge has neither name nor number, nor is it under the jurisdiction of any grand lodge."

We all looked astonished and scared. More than one suspected that a false Mason had managed to obtain admission. The Master said rather sternly:

"Be good enough to explain."

"I was made a Mason among the Chippewa Indians; your committee knows whether it was real or not."

"There can be no question about *that*," promptly spoke one of the committee.

"I have visited fully a score of lodges in the West and East and have never failed of admission wherever I applied."

"It is news to me that there are Masons among the Indians," remarked the Master, voicing the sentiments of the rest of us.

"Why, my dear brother, there are hundreds of them. I

could relate incidents that would amaze you, in which the lives of white men have been spared through the fact that the Indians learned they were Free Masons."

"Are Masons to be found among all the tribes?"

"By no means; only among the most advanced, such as in Indian Territory. I have made the signs without being recognized in scores of instances, and then again, when I had little hope of anything of the kind, help was given me. There were many such instances during the Sioux outbreak in Minnesota, in 1862. I know of an American officer who passed entirely through the line of hostiles armed with a Masonic pass given him by one of the chiefs, who knew of his being a member of the same order with himself."

"Do you have lodge buildings among the Chippewas?" asked the Master.

"No; we always meet on the summit of a high hill, with rows of sentinels, corresponding to our three degrees. It happens now and then that a curious warrior tries to reach the lodge. He may succeed in passing the Entered Apprentice line, but is sure to be discovered by the Fellow Craft sentinels. And," added Brother Jennings, with a significant smile, "he never makes a second attempt to tread on forbidden ground."

"Why not?"

"For the reason that he is invariably put to death. I have seen it done."

The same thought was in the minds of us all; this brother had probably assisted in the exequies of such an intruder.

"How is it with the Apaches?" I inquired.

Our visitor shook his head.

"I don't think you will find any Masons there. Are you especially interested in that tribe, the most terrible in our country?"

"I expect soon to return to my post in the Southwest and to help in forcing Geronimo and some of the others into subjection, and to make them good Indians."

"I'm afraid you will have to use General Sheridan's plan, when he declared that the only good Indian is a dead one. No, my brother, if you ever get into hot quarters in the Southwest, don't count on any help from the order."

After further chat, the lodge was called to labor. The visitor remained through the raising of a fellow craft to the master's degree. He and I talked as we gained chance, and when the lodge broke up, he invited me to call upon him at the Tremont Hotel. I presented myself on the following evening. He received me in his handsome apartments, and confirmed my belief that he was in good circumstances. He had every convenience and luxury at the command of the hotel, smoked the finest cigars and invited me to drink wine, though he did not indulge himself. When I declined, he added:

"I am glad to see it; intoxicants are an unmixed evil. I was once a hard drinker, but for ten years have not tasted a drop, and shall never do so, unless it is in dire necessity and to save my life."

Naturally I was full of curiosity concerning this remarkable man, but did not feel free to question him. He must have known of my feeling, for in the course of conversation he told me considerable about himself.

"I have an Indian name," said he, "which was given me by the Chippewas. It is 'El-tin-wa,' and means 'pale brother.' Of course, I never use it among my own people, though I was strongly tempted to send it in last night to the lodge, instead of that which I received from my parents."

"You have spent a good deal of time among the Indians?"

"Yes; I ran away from home when I was a lad. I had no

intention of staying among the red men, but when our party of emigrants was crossing the plains, we were attacked one dark night by a large band and every one massacred except myself."

"How was it you escaped?"

"I don't know. I was wounded, and I suppose they thought me dead when I was found stretched senseless under one of the wagons. A chief took a fancy to me and carried me away on his horse with him to his home, where I was nursed back to health and strength. He was not a Chippewa, for that tribe lives farther to the north, but his people had friendly relations with the Chippewas, and he turned me over to them. My resolve was to escape on the first opportunity, but that was so long coming that I grew to like my new people and finally settled among them. I became a good hunter, and pleased them so well in several warlike excursions against the Sioux and other tribes, that they made me a chief and christened me, as I have told you, with the name of 'El-tin-wa.' Soon after reaching my majority, I married the daughter of another chief, and two children, a boy and a girl, were born to us."

"Then you will return to the Chippewas?"

He mournfully shook his head.

"Never; wife and both children are dead; the ties that bound me to them are broken forever. I feel no yearning to live with them again, though the whole tribe are my friends. Being free to do as I chose, I came eastward, expecting to spend the rest of my days among my own people. The years with the Chippewas, however, had wrought a change in my nature; I soon tired of the restraints of civilized life. The only relatives I had left were my aged father and a sister. Without telling them my purpose, for I knew how it would sadden them, I quietly left home and again went westward.

I spent some time among the Chippewas, but could not stand it, and began a wandering life, which took me among the Sioux, the Blackfeet and many of the tribes farther south. It was another impulse of my restless state of mind that brought me eastward again to this city, where I had left my father and sister. A woeful disappointment awaited me."

I sympathetically inquired as to what he referred.

"I was prepared to hear of the death of my father, for he was an old man when I left him years before, but it never entered my mind that my sister could be dead. She was buried three years ago."

"Surely you have drunk deep from sorrow's cup," I said, as I noted the moisture in his eye and the sigh that followed his words.

"Yes; sorrow is the lot of man. I haven't a living relative in the wide world; my father and my sister died in good circumstances, so that I have enough to keep me in comfort the rest of my days, but I am like a ship at sea without a rudder."

I could think of little to comfort him. The most that I could do was to suggest that the best remedy in this world for grief is work. The man who keeps his brain and hands actively employed has no time for brooding sorrow.

"There can be no question of the truth of that, and I have thought hard over it, but am unable to fix upon any business toward which I do not feel distaste. It would have been far better for me if my relatives had not left me a penny, though the discovery of a gold mine in the Southwest had made me rich before I came east the last time."

I made a wild venture.

"Why not go westward with me and enlist as a scout in our army? Your knowledge of the country and of Indian ways would be of vast help, for we have a big job on our hands in the subjugation of the Apaches."

I would have given much to know how this strange proposal impressed him. He was sitting beside the table in the middle of the room, his legs crossed, as was his custom, and with one elbow resting on the support. He flung away the remnant of a cigar, took another from the goblet which held several, and lit it with a match from a silver case which he carried, instead of using those in the small box beside the cigars. He puffed for a minute or two, with his eyes fixed not upon me, but upon the upper part of the ceiling on the opposite side of the room. He continued smoking, while I silently waited for him to speak. Instead of doing so, he slowly shook his head. He declined my proposal for reasons, which he did not choose to give. He abruptly asked:

"When do you return to your post?"

"I must leave next week, allowing myself six or eight days to reach Arizona."

"I understood you to say you have taken part in the campaign in the Southwest."

"I have spent two years in that section and found it the hardest kind of work."

"Then you know something of the Apaches?"

"I have a suspicion that I do."

"They are the most terrible tribe in the country. I have travelled among them for weeks at a time. They have been unjustly used by our people, but that is the fact with all Indians with whom we have had trouble. Back of every outbreak and massacre are broken treaties, scoundrelly agents and the lack of honor by our Government. There was no trouble with the Warm Spring Indians until 1872, when the Interior Department was persuaded into ordering them to leave their fertile grounds in Warm Spring Valley, where they were content and happy. They were forcibly shifted to the sterile region around Fort Tularosa. General Howard protested, and had them sent back to their old homes. But the covetous white villains would not let them alone, and a still greater mistake was made when they were sent to the San Carlos Reservation, for not only was the water brackish and the soil worthless, but it was the home of a thousand Chiricahua Apaches, who were the implacable enemies of the Warm Spring band, which hardly numbered three-fourths as many."

"Geronimo is the leader of the Warm Spring Indians?"

"Yes; you will have a frightful time before you subdue *him* and put him where he can do no further harm. I knew his father, Mangus, one of the most fiendish wretches that ever lived. He had no grievance against the white man, but massacred through sheer love of deviltry. He died with his boots or moccasins on, and left his son well trained in the ways of the merciless parent."

Noting how well my friend was informed regarding the Apaches, I asked him several questions, which had puzzled us officers in the Southwest.

"One of the natives that we have enlisted against Geronimo is another chief named Chato. Do you know him?"

"Very well; he is a cousin of Geronimo, and the two profess to be inveterate enemies. Chato was the miscreant who murdered the family of Judge McComas at one of the Gila crossings; then he turned good Indian and has given you much help."

"General Miles once said to me that he never dared fully to trust Chato, though he has not been able to bring home any treacherous act to him. What do you think?"

Again, my friend smoked his cigar for a minute without

speaking, while he gazed thoughtfully at the opposite side of the room.

"I hardly know how to answer your question. There are very few Indians that can be trusted. I have met a few noble characters, but I can't name an Apache who is fireproof. I may be doing Chato injustice, but it seems to me impossible for an Indian who has been as devilish as he to become thoroughly changed. Nothing except a conversion to Christianity will do that. You mustn't be surprised if some day you discover that there is a perfect understanding between Geronimo and Chato, and the Warm Spring leader receives through some means timely warning of all your campaigns against him."

This statement made me uneasy. It was not the first time I had heard it; it was shared by more than one of our officers, and, as I have said, that sagacious leader, General Miles, was not free from distrust. I recalled that I had been on several scouting expeditions with Chato when, had he chosen to play me and my friends false, not one of us would have escaped alive. I weakly dissented from the pessimistic view of my friend.

"I may be in error; he may be honest, but suppose he is waiting for a still better chance to strike you a blow? It is not unlikely that he intends to play the rôle of a friend to the end, for he is a shrewd Indian, and may content himself with getting word to Geronimo when the latter is in danger. The only counsel I have to give you is to be on your guard and don't trust *any* of your Indian scouts or recruits farther than you are forced to trust them."

We chatted in this fashion until quite late. When I rose to bid my new friend goodnight, I accepted his invitation to spend the following evening with him. Evidently, he was well disposed toward me. But a surprise greeted me when

"Don't trust any of your Indian scouts"

I called at the desk and sent my name to his room. He had left that afternoon.

"Where has he gone?" I asked in astonishment.

"He left no word; he simply paid his bill and went to the railway station."

"Is there no word for me?"

The clerk shook his head.

Little did I dream of the circumstances in which El-tin-wa and I were next to meet.

II

GERONIMO was on the warpath again. He had been hunted so persistently that he seemed to believe it would soon be all up with him. He came back to his reservation, declaring he was tired of being an outlaw, and would go on the warpath no more. Few did not receive these pledges with distrust, for that terrible Apache's blood thirst was unquenchable. No matter if, he remained peaceful for years, many would draw their breath in dread. So long as he lived and made his home in the Southwest, no man, woman or child was safe from his fury.

When weeks and months passed without the slightest hostile act on his part, the timid began to hope. During the period named he was a model husband, father and agriculturist. Despite the sterility of the soil, he toiled industriously, he smoked his pipe, he smiled upon his children and the one that happened to be his wife at the time— the old fellow has had seventeen wives at least—and talked pleasantly with the agent and officers who passed the time of day with him. He even seemed to feel a genuine friendship for the men in uniform that had harassed him into submission.

All the same, the majority of us were convinced that, sooner or later, he would raise the mischief again.

Sure enough, one morning in May 1885, Geronimo broke from the reservation, taking with him thirty-four warriors, eight youths and ninety-one women. With the least possible delay, we were in the saddle, and after the fierce horde, though the best mounted of us knew it was impossible to overtake them. The old chief was aware that pursuit would be instant, and his party did not go into camp until they had ridden one hundred and twenty miles. It was clear that he was aiming for the mountains, where every cañon, cave, stream, ravine and even rock was familiar to the band. We pressed our horses to the limit, but did not overtake the renegades, nor get near enough even to exchange shots with them.

We had a dozen of the best Apache scouts with us, and plunged into the mountains under their guidance. Directed by the matchless Vikka, who, despite his fifty-odd years, was as active, wiry, powerful and alert as ever, we ran Geronimo down and made him prisoner, though most of his party got away. It was the chief we were after, and we should rather have caught him than all the rest. He was sullen and defiant, and we felt particularly impatient with him.

"Confound it!" said Captain Swartmore to me; "it wasn't managed right."

"I am not sure I understand you, captain."

"Yes, you do; what's the use of playing off like that? We had it all fixed. Captain Cook or I was to fire off his revolver accidentally when the dusky devil was in the way. We were ready to apologize after he had skipped to his happy hunting grounds, but the whole thing was over, and he had surrendered before we came up."

"You ought to have let some of the rest of us into your secret."

"There shouldn't have been any need of anything like that; America expects every man to do his duty."

"The opportunity was mine. I'm sorry I didn't know of your little arrangement, but next time I'll bear it in mind."

I may remark parenthetically that such "arrangements" are carried out oftener than most folks suppose. For instance, I happen to know of a certainty that it was understood when the party went out from Fort Yates, in December 1890, to arrest Sitting Bull, excuse was to be found for shooting him while "resisting arrest," and it was accordingly so done.

However, Geronimo having been accepted as a prisoner, that was the end of it. We held him that day and night, and then, by gracious! If he did not break away again. More than that, he came back several nights later with several of his best, or rather worst, warriors, entered our camp, went to the tent of one of the officers, seized his wife and whispered to the terrified captive that the only way to save her life was to show him the tent in which his wife was held prisoner. The woman was glad enough to show him, whereupon he set her down, rushed to the right tent, caught up his wife and was off again before any one excepting the woman knew he had been in camp.

Matters were in this exasperating state when that magnificent soldier (afterward killed in the Philippines), Captain Henry W. Lawton, took charge of the immediate campaign against Geronimo. He believed the chief would retreat to his stronghold in the Sierra Madres, south of the Rio Grande. We had an understanding with the Mexican authorities by which permission was given to the soldiers of each country to run down the hostiles on either side of the line. No matter where Geronimo went, we should be after him, and the forces of our sister republic would do all they could to help us.

We had no more than fairly started on our pursuit when news came that Geronimo and his band had not gone to Mexico, but had broken up into small parties, and were raiding, like so many jungle tigers, through Southwestern Arizona and Northwestern Sonora. Lawton thereupon changed his original plan and took up the direct pursuit.

Lawton's command consisted of thirty-five men of Troop B, my own Fourth Cavalry, twenty Indian scouts, and twenty men of Company D, Eighth Infantry, and two packtrains. We left Fort Huachuca early in May, and pressed the pursuit with the utmost vigor in our power.

It was as hot as the hinges of Hades. Never have I experienced such weather as we suffered during the following weeks. In June, fresh detachments of infantry and scouts took the places of those that were worn out, and before the close of the following month we had travelled fourteen hundred miles and the hostiles were driven southeast of Oposura. If we had no rest ourselves, neither had the Apaches. Three different times we burst into their camp, and, abandoning their animals and material, they scattered like quail to cover in the mountains. As Lawton said in his account of the campaign, "Every device known to the Indian was practised to throw me off the trail, but without avail. My trailers were good, and it was soon proved that there was no spot the enemy could reach where security was assured."

When the cavalry succumbed, infantry and Indian scouts took their places. So terrific were the heat and hardships that many of the strongest soldiers gave out, until only fourteen of the infantry were left. When there was not a shoe to the feet of any one, Lieutenant A. L. Smith with his cavalry took their work upon themselves. This incredible pursuit was due to General Miles, who had taken the place of General Crook, relieved at his own request.

It was the privilege of several of us who had been in at the start to stick it out to the end. Among the iron-limbed scouts were a number also who withstood the frightful heat and privations. Chief of those was Vikka, that wonderful Apache, with an eye like the eagles, muscles of steel and an endurance that seemed not to know the meaning of fatigue. Often I looked at him as he rode his gaunt pony, without saddle, at my side and envied the salamander that seemed to revel in the furnace-like temperature. Frequently the fingers of the men were blistered by contact with the iron of their weapons. Many times, when we had struggled on to some well-known spring or water hole, we found it either dry or so befouled by the hostiles that had been ahead of us that one would have died of thirst before touching the water. Our poor horses suffered with us, and more than one succumbed, not so much from exhaustion as from thirst. There were times when we would have welcomed the muddiest pool that could hold the fluid in solution like iced nectar. We seemed to become mere automata, moving without will of our own, but held to the fearful work by a blind, aimless, dogged persistency that nothing but death could stop.

The throbbing afternoon was well advanced when Vikka and I reined up our ponies on the edge of a stretch of sand that was hot enough to roast eggs. A mile or more to the westward loomed a mountain spur, whose blue tint throbbed in the flaming sunshine, as if it were the phantasmagora of a disordered brain. The Apache trail led in that direction, and we were morally sure that Geronimo and his band were gathered there, unless, with that persistency which was a feature of their retreat, they had pressed through and were fleeing into the broken region beyond. We had pushed our horses to the limit, and Lieutenant Smith halted the command among the hills not far to the rear of where my dusky companion and I paused to scan the white, blistering sand that stretched away to the mountain spur. By permission of the officer, Vikka and I had ridden this comparatively short distance, and it rested with us whether we should advance any farther toward the enemy.

This expanse of plain was a bed of sand that pulsated in the intolerable sunlight. It was ridged and hummocky in many places, having been thus twisted and flirted about by the gusts of wind that sometimes played pranks with the mobile stuff. Not so much as a shrivelled cactus or yellow spear of grass showed; it was a scene of horrible waste and desolation from which one would shrink as from the core of Death Valley itself.

Vikka checked his pony directly at my side, and we peered across the fiery waste at the cool-looking spur in the distance. The sweat on our animals was baked dry. How we stood it is beyond my comprehension, but a man can become accustomed almost to anything. A few months previous, a half hour's exposure to such merciless heat would have tumbled me headlong from my saddle with sunstroke; but I had ridden for hours through this hellish temperature and felt no special ill effects. The point seemed to have been reached where the dull body becomes inured and insensible to that which in ordinary circumstances would be fatal.

I looked across at Vikka. His dirty, luxuriant hair dangled about his shoulders, but he was without the slightest head covering. Not so much as a feather showed among his horsehair like locks. That skull must have withstood a hundred degrees, but it mattered nothing to him. Not a drop of moisture showed on the rough, bronzed features, though if it had appeared it probably would have evaporated in a flash. He was scantily clothed, but I presume it would have been all the same to him if one of the dirty blankets of his tribe swathed his shoulders. He wore leggins and strong moccasins, and, as I have said, rode his pony without saddle and with only a halter. He needed nothing more. Many times, I had admired the physique of this remarkable man. He was over six feet tall and as symmetrical as a Greek statue. He was immensely powerful, but, like his entire race, showed only a moderate muscular development. His endurance was incredible. I have known him to scout for thirty-six hours in succession, during which his mental faculties were keyed to the highest point, and yet he appeared as bright and alert as if just roused from sleep. General Crook has said that any one of the Apaches would lope for fifteen hundred feet up the side of a mountain, and at the end, you could not observe the slightest increase of respiration. I have known Vikka to do it time and again, without the first evidence of what he had passed through.

This remarkable Apache spoke English quite well, and sometimes he told me of his past life. He had been one of the most implacable miscreants that served under Mangus, and there is no question that he had committed shuddering deeds of atrocity, but he had a bitter quarrel with Geronimo, and hated him and all the hostiles with an unquenchable hatred.

Now and then when on that last campaign in the Southwest, in which we ran the Apache leader to earth, I would suddenly recall the warning that Jared Jennings spoke to me when spending the evening with him at his hotel. "Never trust *any* Indian," was its substance, and he added that the race were capable of pretending friendship for years, with the unfaltering purpose of seizing the best opportunity for biting the hand that fed them.

So it was that more than once when in special peril, I asked myself whether it was safe fully to trust Vikka. It would seem that he had already served the United States so well, and had struck so many blows against his people, that, if he meditated treachery, he could never atone for these acts. I recalled that on more than one occasion I had trusted him so fully that he could have brought about my death without causing a shadow of suspicion. When I thought of all this, I compressed my lips and muttered, "I will never doubt *him;* he has been tested by fire."

And yet the old, vague, tormenting suspicion would come to me, and it came again when I glanced sideways at him, and saw his black eyes gazing off across the shimmering plain toward the mountain spur. The misgiving was unreasonable, but it would not down. I shuddered as I reflected that when he should bound back to barbarism and his own natural self, his first victim must be me. Why did he wait so long before striking? Was he planning some huge treason that would overwhelm us all?

Hardly had I asked myself the question when I flung it aside, impatient that I had allowed it a momentary lodgment in my thoughts. "He is the type of faithfulness. I have trusted him with my life and will do so again whenever it is necessary."

I raised the glass, which I carried slung about my neck, and levelled it at the elevations in the distance. Brought out more clearly, I noted the high hill in the foreground, and the gray rocks and stunted pines. Another lower peak rose to the right a little farther back, while the crown of a third showed faintly beyond. The intense heat caused a throbbing of the air, which made the objects flicker and dance in one's vision. Naught that resembled animal life was discerned. It was as inert and dead as at the morn of creation.

Then I carefully studied the white, lumpy sand that stretched between. Not even a rattlesnake or insect could be seen wriggling at our feet. I lowered the glass and offered it to Vikka. He shook his head. I never knew him to use such help, for his keenness of vision was marvellous.

"See 'Pache?" he asked, in his sententious fashion.

"No; I can't catch sight of hide or hair of them, but no doubt they are among the hills and watching us."

"I see 'Pache!" was his startling remark.

"Where?" I demanded, whipping up the glass again. "I know you have mighty good eyes, Vikka, but I ought to do as well as you with the telescope."

"Don't look right place; ain't in hills—closer by."

It was an astonishing declaration. If the hostiles were not among the mountains, where could they be? Surely, this plain of pulsing sand could not hide them without so much as a shrub and hardly a blade of withered grass. Lowering the glass, I looked inquiringly at my companion. The iron countenance was wrinkled with a smile, which showed his even white teeth. I saw that he was not looking at the hills, but at the plain a short way out. What did he see there? Was not this a display of the waggery, which he showed at rare intervals? Was he not having a little amusement at my expense?

But it was no time for jest; the scout was in earnest. He certainly had discovered *something*. Without raising a hand to point, and speaking in a low voice, he said:

"The 'Paches are close; they have laid ambush."

Thus directed, I studied the plain without the aid of the glass. No more than a hundred yards away, I now noted a series of hillocks. They numbered nearly a score. While they bore a general resemblance to other lumps visible in every part of the plain, these were grouped together more compactly. Leading out from where we had halted, the trail of Geronimo's band passed within a few rods, so that had our command kept to the tracks, we must have ridden in front of them.

Every hillock of flaming sand hid the body of an Apache. Those terrible miscreants would grovel in the fiery dirt with every part of the body covered and only the serpentlike eyes peering out and fixed upon the white men. Unsuspicious of anything of the kind, nothing would have been more natural than for us to ride quietly past. Then when our faces were turned away, a jet of fire would spout from each hummock, and half our saddles would be emptied. That very thing has been done more than once in the Indian campaigning in the Southwest.

But Vikka penetrated the subtle trick. Had he failed to do so, his career and mine would have terminated within the following few minutes. Did I need any further proof of his fidelity?

"You are right, Vikka," I said in a low voice. "I see where they are hiding; it won't do for us to go a step nearer them. I think it best we should dash back, for we are nigh enough for them to pick us off as it is."

It was then the dusky scout did a daring thing. He brought his rifle to his shoulder, and taking quick aim, let fly at the nearest hummock. A rasping screech followed, showing that the dusky desperado crouching beneath was hit hard. At the same instant, from every other sand heap a frowsy buck leaped upright, the grains streaming from his dirty clothes like rain, while their war shrieks cut the air. From each hideous exudation issued, a tongue of flame and every bullet was aimed at us.

But there had been no pause on our part. Hardly had Vikka pressed the trigger, then he wheeled his pony and dashed off on a dead run. I was not a second behind in doing the same, and each threw himself forward on his animal, else, we could hardly have escaped the storm of bullets that whistled over and about us. Had they aimed at our horses, we must have been dismounted, but before they could repair their mistake, we were beyond range. Glancing over my shoulder, I saw the frowsy figures running full speed after us, loading and firing as best they could, but our ponies were accustomed to sudden demands upon their energies, and they quickly carried us out of danger. My second glance showed they were loping toward the mountain spur, where doubtless Geronimo and his hostiles were awaiting the result of the attempt to ambuscade us. But they had failed, and fearing pursuit, were speeding across the plain beyond reach of the avenging cavalry.

"I wish," said I, when we drew our animals down to a walk, as we approached the cover where Lieutenant Smith and the command had halted for rest, "that all our men could have stopped where we did."

Vikka looked across at me in a way that showed he did not understand my meaning.

"Instead of riding past the hummocks of sand, we could have charged and routed out the devils, picking them off as they showed themselves."

The scout shook his head.

"*I* knew where to aim; rest of soldiers would not; sand keep off their bullets; 'Paches shoot first."

"That might be, but they would have been at disadvantage, and we should have made the trick cost them dear."

The fellow was not impressed by my idea. When I came to reflect upon it, I saw he was right. If, instead of riding calmly past the prostrate figures in the sand we should have galloped straight at them, they would have been taken by surprise, but such fellows are never at a loss what to do. Brief as was the intervening distance, every mother's son of them would have fired before we could reach them, and with appalling results to us. Even if we had first emptied our carbines, it was more likely, as Vikka had said that most of our shots would have proved ineffective, for there was enough sand enclosing each of the Apaches to screen their bodies.

"Vikka," said I abruptly, "suppose you became a prisoner of Geronimo, what would he do with you?"

A broad grin lit up the bronzed visage.

"Vikka will not be prisoner."

"You can't be sure of that; that chief is a fearful fighter and you take many chances; some day you may fall into his hands."

"Vikka *never* be prisoner," repeated my companion. Then I understood his meaning. Knowing the feeling of the leader of the Warm Spring Indians toward him, Vikka would simply take his own life when he saw all hope was gone.

That thing has been done many a time in the Southwest by white men, women and even by Indians themselves.

III

THE halting place among the hills offered such advantages that Lieutenant Smith turned them to account. Men and animals had been pressed to the limit of endurance, and none ever needed rest more than they. The fleeing Apaches had been pushed so relentlessly that they did not pause to contaminate the spring, where we stopped, dismounted, drank and filled our canteens. The water not only gave the ponies all they could drink, but nourished a species of lush grass, upon which the animals fed eagerly. We ate, lolled on the ground, smoked our pipes and the majority slept. Even

Vikka and I had snatched brief slumber before riding out on our little scout.

When Lieutenant Smith had heard my report, he called Vikka, Pedro, Jim and others of the best scouts around him for consultation. Chato at that time was not with us. We cavalrymen were so few in number, and all so personally interested in everything, that those who did not prefer to sleep joined the group, of which I was a member.

We were on the direct trail of Geronimo and his band, and with such skillful trackers as we had with us, it was impossible for the hostiles to throw us off the scent. We had but to press on across the plain into the mountain spur, when we should be upon their heels.

And right there rose the problem, and a mighty serious one it was, too. If we pushed over the sandy waste, the fugitives could not fail to discover our pursuit. They could scatter among the rocks and fastnesses, or, what seemed more likely, set a series of traps, which, with all the skill of our scouts, it would be hardly possible for us to avoid.

What Lieutenant Smith sought to learn was the "lay of the country" beyond the mountain spur. That was readily ascertained from Vikka and others. The delicate question was whether our scouts could reason out the destination of Geronimo—not his ultimate destination, which probably the wily devil did not know himself, but the point where he would halt that night, or at the furthest, the following night. Then, instead of keeping to the trail, we should take a circuitous course and reach the spot ahead of the hostiles, and wait for them; or, if that was not feasible, we could be there in time to surprise them.

The advantage of such strategy was apparent. It must be overwhelmingly in our favor, and would enable us to strike the most effective blow yet delivered in our pursuit, covering many hundred miles. The whole thing hinged upon the right selection of the destination of the hostiles. If we should mistake, or they should detect our scheme, we should be miles off the right course and must lose several precious days, when every hour was of the last importance.

But right there an unexpected difficulty confronted us. Vikka, Pedro and Jim agreed that Geronimo was heading for the Wolf Mountains, a range twenty miles to the south. If he succeeded in reaching them with his women and children, it would prove an almost impossible task to run them to earth, though every one of us was as determined as ever to do so. It would be a big thing if we could head them off, or, what would be equally decisive, surprise them among those fastnesses. To do so it was necessary for us to leave the trail and reach the Wolf Mountains by a roundabout course, and this could not be undertaken until later in the day, since the shelter furnished by our own range would serve for only a short distance.

The difficulty to which I allude was this: All the scouts, with one exception, believed that Geronimo was already on his way to the point named. That exception was Vikka, who insisted that he would stay where he was, in the hope of ambuscading the cavalry, and he would resume his flight on the morrow, probably early in the morning. Therefore, if we intended to strike a blow at night, it must be done within a mile or two of our present camp. No argument could shake the conviction of Vikka on this point.

Lieutenant Smith was puzzled. Here was one man against a dozen. True, Vikka had no superior, but among the others were several who were his equal, and it would seem that when they united, their logic ought to outweigh that of a single man, be he never so cunning and wise. Moreover, as it appeared to the rest of us, common sense was against Vikka.

The Apache leader had been taught long before that, there was no rest for his feet, and that his only safety lay in rapid and continued flight. What reason, then, was there for the hostiles remaining near our camp, when they ran great risk in doing so?

Smith took me aside.

"Lieutenant," said he, "I'll be hanged if I know what's best to do. What do you think of things?"

"I am as much puzzled as you. You know my faith in Vikka. He and I have been on more than one dangerous scout, and I have never met his superior. He saved my life this afternoon, and has not once failed me; I feel like tying to him."

"Even in *this* instance?"

"I'm not sure. I noticed that when you asked him his reasons for believing Geronimo would stay where he is until to-morrow he refused to tell them."

"More than that, he acted as if he were offended. I don't see why he should be unreasonable, as he certainly is in this instance."

I made no reply to this, for, as I have said, I was as much mystified as Smith himself. We were standing apart from the rest, and the lieutenant leaned his elbow on the rock beside him. He thoughtfully smoked his pipe for a minute or two, gazing at the ground in a way I had often seen him do when pondering some question. Suddenly he looked up and asked in a whisper, just loud enough for me to hear:

"Lieutenant, have you ever felt any distrust of Vikka?"

The question fairly took me off my feet. I tried to parry.

"How can I suspect him after to-day and the other times in which he has given proof of his loyalty?"

"You haven't answered my question."

"Some time ago a man who had spent most of his life among the Indians warned me never to trust any one of them. I am ashamed to say I *have* felt a touch of misgiving concerning Vikka, and I felt it to-day, but it was before he saved my life."

With his keen eyes still fixed on my face, Smith added:

"Do you believe he is honest in saying Geronimo will stay where he is until tomorrow?"

"I do."

"So do I, and I shall act upon that view. We will follow the ridge to the north, keeping it between us and the hostiles, and then enter the mountains above where the old devil will be looking for us. We shall have a moon to-night, but there will be plenty of clouds."

"What of rain?"

The lieutenant looked about and up into the sky. There had been deluges of dishwater five nights out of seven for the last month. This was well enough in its way, for we were able to keep our canteens filled, but it was anything but comfortable for us. We kindled no fires, for it was too dangerous, and despite the terrific heat of the day, the nights were often chilly. It had not rained for forty-eight hours, and probably a season of drought was on us.

"I don't think we shall have rain. This part of the world looks as if there had not been any downfall for a month. We shall be able to set out with our canteens full, while every man and horse at the start will be a barrel himself. I say, lieutenant, you and Vikka have been chums ever since we left the fort."

"I admit that I have a fondness for him and he seems to like me."

"Well, one word; keep a special eye on him. You will

have a better chance than any one else, he may have been playing for the opening that is coming to-night. At the first proof of treachery on his part——"

"I understand," I interrupted. "I'll do it."

The rest, which we gained among these hills, did a world of good. We had halted about noon, and it was five or six hours later when we rode slowly to the north, with the ridge between us and the spur, among which we believed the hostiles were watching for our coming. Our Indian scouts kept well in advance and could be counted upon to give timely warning. It was certain that the Apaches had some of their own scouts out, and the utmost caution was necessary on our part to elude detection. In the latter case, we were sure to have our trouble for naught, with the prospect that the cunning enemy would turn the tables upon us.

Night had already closed in when we reached a point some three miles away, where it was our plan to turn to the westward, with a view of getting among the hills, in which we figured that Geronimo and his band were on the alert against surprise. By this time it was certain we should have no rain. The night proved what Lieutenant Smith had anticipated. The sky contained many tumbling clouds slowly moving across, and showing the twinkling stars in the clear spaces. The moon was nearly full, but would not rise until well toward midnight, or "low twelve." This was in our favor, for we counted upon the absence of clear light to screen our advance.

As before, the scouts held well in front, while we with our horses on a walk moved as silently as possible. Debouching from the rugged region, we entered upon the plain, where the ponies' hoofs sank into the spongy sand with the faintest possible noise. Among the twenty-odd cavalrymen hardly a word was spoken. All were listening and peering into the gloom as it parted to make room for us. We hardly expected to see anything wrong, but the faint bird-like call of one or more of the scouts was likely to pierce the stillness at any moment. I kept pretty close to the side of my superior officer, whose senses were on the alert. He had proved his intrepidity as well as his coolness in critical situations, and though I had gone out on more personal scouts than he had, I relied upon his judgment at all times. Nature and education had given him a wealth of mental resources that always stood him in good stead.

Suddenly through the soft hush came the soft tremolo, which we were expecting. It was the signal from the scouts for us to halt. Our horses seemed to understand the warning, for most of them paused without the gentle pressure of the rein. Still no one spoke. We were waiting for the second signal, which never failed to be sent after a proper interval. The first might miscarry, and it would not do to run the risk of a thing like that.

The interval was no more than two or three minutes, when the call reached us again. We knew it would not be repeated, for in the circumstances it was impossible that both signals should fail. The orders thus far were for us to halt and wait. If the crisis were such that we should fall back, the signal for that would follow. It did not, and we sat silent in our saddles, peering fixedly into the gloom, where we expected our dusky friends to show themselves.

Instead of coming from that direction, the shadowy forms took shape to our left. First, there was one, then two loomed into sight, and then the others appeared. The whole party had been sent out, and was now among us again, Vikka being the first that was recognized.

The report showed that the sagacious fellow had been right in his surmise. Geronimo and his band had been located about a fourth of a mile away among the hills, and had gone into camp in a small basin-like valley, where there were water and grass. The disposition of the men and women showed that the hostiles were ready and probably expecting an attack. If the cavalry followed the most obvious course among the mountains, they must pass near the depression, in which the Apaches were awaiting them. Could the latter effectually conceal themselves, the ambush must prove as disastrous as that in the open plain would have been to me but for the timely warning of my companion.

Never was more subtle cunning and patience matched against each other than in the pursuit and flight of Geronimo and his band that had broken away from the reservation. Some of the exploits on both sides were so incredible that they would not be believed if told. Truth forces one to say that there never would have been the slightest chance of success on the part of the United States cavalry but for the help given by the native scouts. Matched against their own race, it was simply "Greek meeting Greek." One was as much an adept in woodcraft as the other. Sometimes our men failed because the others were the wiser in certain contingencies. Again, it was the other way. All this backed up by an indomitable, remorseless pursuit, such as had never been seen before, fixed the end from the beginning.

It is hard to understand the marvellous skill with which several of our scouts had discovered the Apache camp without being observed in turn by the sentinels who were on the watch. Lieutenant Smith frankly told Vikka and the two companions, Pedro and Jim, who had made this daring venture, that success on their part—that is, without being detected in turn—was out of the question. Nevertheless, the trio spoke with such quiet assurance that the lieutenant was compelled to believe them.

Thus far, everything had gone as well as we could hope. We had located the camp of the hostiles without revealing ourselves. All now depended upon the manner in which we carried out the remaining part of the momentous programme.

With the cavalry and scouts—the latter of course being on foot, we having taken their ponies in charge—grouped irregularly around, we held a council of war, in which all felt a freedom in expressing his opinion not often seen in a military company.

The situation may be summed up, thus: The Apaches whom we had been chasing for weeks were known to be camped hardly a fourth of a mile away, in a basin among the rugged fastnesses of the mountain spur. They would remain there until dawn, in the hope of taking us at a vast disadvantage. If nothing of the kind occurred, they would resume their flight at the earliest streaking of daylight. Their scouts were not only watching the path which we were likely to follow, but, as a matter of course, were guarding their camp from every side.

Matters being thus, could we steal upon them from an unexpected direction, bursting like a cyclone into their camp and taking prisoners or wiping out the whole band? How eagerly every one of us hoped that such might be the issue! It would mark the end of this awful campaigning and our return to civilization.

All the scouts agreed with Vikka that the chance of success was good enough to justify the attempt. We should certainly accomplish something, even if the bucks took the alarm before we could rush their camp. Lieutenant Smith decided to attack.

That being so, the precise course to be followed had yet to be settled. It was necessary to leave our animals at the foot of the hills, where something like shelter could be secured.

Three men were to remain to look after them, while the others stole toward the camp of the redskins.

It should be said, further, that the expectation was to make the attack just before daybreak. That is the favorite hour with Indians themselves, for it marks the lowest ebb of one's vitality and alertness. Despite the vigilance of the sentinels, thrown out on every side by the hostiles, some of the latter would be asleep. Incredible as was their endurance, it had nonetheless its limits set. True, they would wake with the suddenness of she-wolves, but by that time, we hoped to be among them, attending to "business."

The plan of approach having been agreed upon, Vikka, Pedro, and Jim moved forward again, with us troopers following at a distance of a hundred yards or so. The purpose of the three was to find the avenue for attack. It was natural that one side or the other of the camp was more vulnerable than the others were. It might be that the sentinel at that point could be stolen upon and despatched so suddenly that he would have no chance to warn the others. We could dash through the opening thus gained and be in the camp in a twinkling.

We used two hours in our stealthy advance, and then, as agreed upon beforehand, halted until notice was received from the scouts, who were near the enemy. No shadows could have moved more noiselessly than we could. Every man of us had been trained in this species of woodcraft, and knew that a careless step, the knocking loose of a small stone even, a word spoken in an undertone, or the rattle of a weapon might give the alarm and bring our whole scheme to naught.

Lieutenant Smith and I were crouching beside a huge rock, slightly farther along than the rest of the men. Bending his head close to mine, he whispered:

"Lieutenant, this is the crisis that will test Vikka."

"I am thinking the same. Shall I steal ahead and see what I can see?"

"I hate to have you run the risk."

"I'll do it."

I slipped off my sword for fear it would betray me and grasped my revolver. I was likely to need it with the suddenness of lightning, and did not mean to be taken unawares.

Smith would have been glad to whisper a word of counsel or at least to say good-by, but it was not necessary or worth the risk.

As I emerged from behind the rock, I perceived that the moon had risen and was rapidly climbing the sky. Just then, it was obscured by a heavy cloud, but observing that it would soon pass, I improved the chance to creep forward for several rods. Then the flood of light was such that I lay flat awaiting another opportunity, which I perceived would soon come.

Ahead of me and slightly to the left towered another boulder, not as large as the one that screened Lieutenant Smith. I crawled behind this and then awaited the obscuration of the moon, to advance farther into the open.

I was in the act of creeping forward, when, without the slightest sound or warning, the figure of an Indian warrior rose to view beside the boulder. One glance at it was enough. I was too familiar with the fellow to be mistaken. It was Geronimo himself.

IV

THE first look was enough. Geronimo, the ferocious leader of the Warm Spring band, was standing within thirty feet of where I lay on my face behind the boulder, with my revolver tightly grasped in my right hand.

"It was Geronimo himself"

My muscles were iron, my nerve cool and the shot a fair one. I had the drop on him and swore he should not escape me.

My second impulse was not to wait, but to bring him down before he turned his head to scan his surroundings. But there was something in such an act at which I revolted. Unspeakable wretch though he was, and deserving of death ten times over, I shrank from a cold-blooded snuffing out of the Apache leader. No, I should wait and give him the shadow of a chance.

I have said that the smothering heat of the days was followed by chilliness at night, which was one of our greatest trials on that memorable campaign. The grim chieftain had a blanket about his shoulders, as if he needed it for comfort. As he stood, his side was toward me and his rough, irregular profile was thus brought out plainly.

The strained situation had lasted no more than a minute when it became plain to me that Geronimo had come here to meet some one. His attitude was that of expectancy, and with his entire wonderful faculties alert, he was peering fixedly a little to the left, from which direction his visitor probably was to advance.

All doubt on this point was removed when from that point a second form came out of the gloom, with no more noise than that made by the shadow of the cloud, which glided over the hills. My heart beat faster than before, for the instant thought was that the chief had moved out from his camp to meet one of our scouts, who was bearing him news of our movements. Such treachery had aided him more than once to escape from critical situations, and now it was about to occur again.

My anxiety was to identify the traitor. I preferred to shoot him rather than the dusky leader, but I compressed my lips with the resolve to make both bite the dust. It would be something to tell in after years that I had brought down Geronimo and the miscreant who was serving him in our own camp.

To my chagrin, the second arrival was not only enclosed in a blanket, but it was drawn so far up around his shoulders that his face was hidden. Only the crown of black, coarse hair showed. Not a feature was visible. Halting within a couple of paces of the chief, the two began conversing in low tones. Their voices were so faint that I could not distinguish a word, and, had I been able to do so, it would have done no good, for naturally they talked in their own language.

The position of the two was such that the side of each showed clearly. They would have to turn their heads at right angles to see my forehead and eyes before they flitted back out of sight. Their training, the strained situation and the peculiar peril in which both stood convinced me that they would neglect no precaution, however slight. Geronimo could have been no more anxious to avoid being seen by our scouts than was the traitor to hide his identity from all except the arch leader of the hostiles.

Incredible as it may seem, neither of these veterans turned his eyes in my direction during the few minutes they talked. My plan was simple. I shifted slightly to rest the weight of my body on my left elbow. This gave freedom of the other arm, and I had but to lift my weapon a few inches to bring the wretches within range. First the traitor, then the Apache chieftain, and before either could know his danger.

I expected every moment that the scout would lower his blanket and show his face. I could think of no reason why he should wish to shroud his features when the countenance of Geronimo was as clearly revealed as if the sun were shining.

But he remained muffled, and I did not see so much as the tip of his nose.

Suddenly a denser cloud than usual swept over the face of the moon. That which had been illuminated was quickly hidden in gloom. The two forms dissolved and faded from sight. Glancing at the orb in the sky, I saw that it would soon emerge from behind the mists. I decided that the second it did so, and my aim was clear, I should let fly at the couple in instant succession.

But that obscuring cloud played the mischief with this plan. When the light began increasing and my straining vision made out the boulder beside which the Apaches were standing less than a minute before, only one was in sight. Geronimo had vanished as silently as he had entered the field of vision.

The other was standing as before, and seemed to be looking after the chief, who had not yet passed from his view. Only for an instant did he do this, when he turned to move away. With his back toward the chief, he lowered the blanket a few inches—just enough to show his countenance, whose profile was toward me. The traitor was Vikka!

I was dumfounded, for, curiously enough, during the brief interval, and despite my recent talk with Lieutenant Smith, it had not occurred to me that the wretch could be he whom each of us had distrusted more than once. By the time I rallied from my speechlessness, he was gone.

The situation was critical to the last degree. I was in advance of our own men, and without further hesitation, I rose to my feet, and in a crouching position ran back to where I had left Lieutenant Smith.

He, too, was on his feet, and the forms of the troopers came rapidly to view, as, in response to a signal, they gathered round him. Among them could be seen in the obscurity several of our scouts. I glanced from face to face, but missed two—Vikka and Pedro. I longed to tell our commandant what I had learned, but could not do so in the hearing of the company. Smith was issuing his commands in low, hurried tones.

"An opening has been made; we're to rush the camp; is every man ready?"

The whispered responses showed that they were ready and eager.

"We will follow Jim; he will lead; all ready!"

The next minute we were threading our way among the boulders, rocks and gullies. I caught up my sword, and hurriedly fastened it on while joining the procession, which was led by the faithful Jim. As yet, I had not spoken to the commander, but now I twitched his elbow.

"I fear we have been betrayed, lieutenant."

"It can't be; come on; it's too late to stop now."

Less than a hundred yards farther the scout Jim uttered a suppressed exclamation and came to a halt. We were around him the next second. Stretched at his feet lay Pedro dead, the wound in the upper part of the breast showing that he had been killed by a single blow with a knife.

The pause was only for a moment, when, with no further attention to the stark form, Jim led the advance at a rapid pace. The moonlight was uncertain. We were close to the deep basin in which clustered the camp of the hostiles. A few steps more, and we came upon a second figure stretched out on the earth. It was that of the Apache sentinel, who had been stricken down so suddenly that he had no chance to give the alarm. This was the opening through which we were to rush, and we did so with scarcely a second's halt.

As the troopers scrambled, leaped and ran they shouted their battle cry. Down the slope they streamed, some of them stumbling and falling, but they were quickly on their feet again, ardent as ever. Within the same minute that we started the rush, we were in the basin hunting like bloodhounds for our prey.

Then a discovery was made as startling as it was exasperating. Brief as was the time used, the Apaches had taken the alarm and fled. The camp was deserted. They had had their warning, and a few minutes, even seconds, were sufficient.

Vikka, coming from somewhere, was among our scouts, two of whom dashed across the basin like a cyclone. We saw the flashes of guns and heard fierce cries. They had come upon the rear guard, so to speak, and we were having it out with them. Among the troopers who were skurrying here and there, baffled and enraged at their failure to find any foes, a half dozen rushed to the help of the scouts. I joined them. We had but a few rods to run, when we struck the farther side of the basin. But we were too late to have any part in the fray. After the exchange of a few shots, in which one of our scouts was wounded and one of the enemy brought down, the others made off swiftly in the darkness and were beyond reach.

As we came together in the gloom, we were a disappointed and furious lot. Angry mutterings were going on; when Smith noticed that one of the Apaches who had fallen was struggling to get to his feet. The scout Jim observed it, and ran forward to finish him with his knife, but the lieutenant was the nearer and stayed his hand.

"He is a prisoner. We don't kill captives, even if they're Apaches."

Seizing the fellow by the arm, he helped him to rise. He was badly hurt, but with the slight aid thus given, was able to stand erect. He looked defiantly around in the faces of his captors as revealed in the moonlight, which was now bright, but did not speak.

"Do any of you know him?" asked the officer, turning to the scouts.

"He is Martaña," replied Vikka; "he is as bad as Geronimo."

All of us had heard that name. He was a sub-chief of the Warm Spring Indians, and one of the most ferocious miscreants that ever helped to ravage the frontier.

"It makes no difference," said the officer sternly; "he seems to have stopped one or two of your bullets and won't make any more trouble for some time to come. No matter how bad he is, I'll shoot the first one who harms him further."

It was useless to attempt to overtake the hostiles during the darkness, and with our scouts thrown out to prevent surprise, we made our way back to camp, where we had left our horses in charge of three of the troopers. Our plan had failed because at the critical juncture Geronimo received warning of the danger to himself and band.

We disposed of ourselves for the remainder of the night. As soon as we could see, the pursuit would be resumed and pressed as vigorously as before. The Indian scouts were kept at work among the hills, to prevent anything in the nature of a surprise by the Apaches, some of whom were likely to steal back in the hope of striking us an unexpected blow.

Our captive Martaña was treated with more consideration than he deserved. A blanket was spread on the ground, upon which he partly reclined. We had no regular surgeon with us at that time, but Lieutenant Smith and several others possessed a practical knowledge of wounds, and gave it as their opinion, that, though the fellow was desperately hurt, he had a chance of pulling through. He was offered food and drink, but refused to touch them. He even knocked aside a whiskey flask that was held to his lips. He could not be persuaded to speak a word, and paid not the least attention to the Apaches who addressed him in his own language. He was a stoic, who shrank from nothing before him. He hated us with an unspeakable hatred. Despite the kindness, we had shown him, he would have scalped every one had the chance been his.

Leaving him to himself, Lieutenant Smith drew me aside as before, and lighting his inevitable pipe, as he sat with his knees drawn up, asked me to explain the hurried words I had spoken just before the charge upon the deserted camp. I did so, he listening and puffing in silence. After a time he said in his low, even voice:

"You told me that in the same instant that you received proof of Vikka's guilt you would shoot him."

"I did say so, but I was literally paralyzed for the moment, not dreaming of anything of the kind; I'm sorry I let him escape."

"So am I, for the evidence you saw was enough to hang him. And yet after all is said, lieutenant, I don't understand that fellow."

"In what respect?"

"He has had no end of chances to strike us the hardest kind of blows, but never did so until to-night. Why should he sacrifice so many greater for the single less?"

"Meaning that his opportunity to-night was less than many others which he let slip?"

"Precisely. What he has just done was negative; he prevented us from surprising Geronimo, but the most that he did for the hostiles was to give them a chance to get away. Why did he not plan a surprise of *us* by *them?* He could have done that very thing three nights ago, in Antelope Pass.

"He may have feared he ran too much risk. He has been

playing a hard part, as you can understand, for he must be under the observation of his own scouts most of the time, and some of them are beyond suspicion."

"I wonder whether he has any partners in this," muttered the officer, as if speaking to himself. "It's blamed uncomfortable to think so."

"Where is he now, lieutenant?"

"He and Jim and several others are scouting among the hills."

"Begging pardon, Vikka ought not to be with them."

"He would not have been had you told me this before. It is best, however, to show no distrust of the fellow till we catch him with the goods."

"Lieutenant, I don't feel the need of sleep. I had enough this afternoon to last me for a good while. With your permission, I'll take a look among the hills myself, hoping to pick up a point or two."

"I don't know as I have any objection. I understand that you will give most of your attention to Vikka?"

"Such is my purpose."

"You haven't one chance in a thousand. He is too cunning to be entrapped by a man who is but a child compared to him."

"I got the best of him this evening."

"Hardly; but if so, it was an accident."

"Another accident may occur."

"If he has any idea that you are onto his game, you will be in tenfold greater danger than ever before. Well, good luck go with you."

When I had reached a point fairly beyond our camp I was impressed for the first time with the absurdity of the task taken upon myself. I had set out to circumvent one of the most skilful trailers and scouts in the service. My woodcraft as compared to his was foolishness. He could give me cards and spades and beat me every time. True, he was somewhere in these hills, but I might prowl among them for a week without getting sight of him. An unprecedented piece of luck had brought me knowledge some time before, but such accidents are never repeated, or, at least, not often enough to justify hope on my part.

Nonetheless, I had no thought of turning back. If I could not outwit Vikka, I might have a chance to do something else. It was in accordance with Apache customs that some of their scouts would linger in the rear of the main band to learn our intentions, and, if opportunity offered, strike us a blow. They knew the pursuit would be taken up in the morning. We were better mounted than they were. In fact, we had scattered the hostiles so often that most of them were on foot. Encumbered with women and children, they were put to it as never before to keep out of our reach. It was, therefore, of the highest importance that they should delay our pursuit whenever possible. By leaving a dozen, more or less, of their best scouts behind, within communicating distance, we might be checked sufficiently to give the main body a chance to increase the distance between them and us.

It was the province of our guides to frustrate these plans, and I was in the mood to take a hand in the desperate business, though common sense dictated that Lieutenant Smith should have prevented such rashness on my part.

I followed a course that led me to the edge of the basin down which we had charged into the deserted camp, and it was with a curious shock that I recognized the very spot where I had seen Geronimo emerge from the gloom and hold his confab with Vikka, when he joined him a few moments later.

"Strange!" I muttered; "if there is anything in signs, I

should accept this as indicating that something of the kind is going to happen again."

There are few of us whose experience has not proved the existence within this marvellous make-up of ours of something akin to that vague faculty which has been called the sixth sense. On no other theory can many things be explained.

I had held my crouching posture only a minute or so when the absolute certainty came over me that some one was near. I glanced in every direction and listened intently, but did not see nor hear the slightest thing that could explain my feeling. Nonetheless, the conviction was unalterable, and rather increased than diminished.

"It can't be that Vikka is prowling here; probably one of Geronimo's scouts is on the lookout, or perhaps one of our own."

What to do was the question that puzzled me. I might steal forward, backward or to one side, and thereby do the very thing I should not do. Surely, some clue must come within a few seconds that would guide me.

As before, I held my revolver ready for instant use. My sword was with me, and I may claim to be an expert in its use, but where was my enemy?

As suddenly, as if an avalanche had descended upon me, I was crushed to earth by a mountainous weight, my senses vanished and all became darkness and oblivion.

V

I DON'T suppose I was unconscious for more than five minutes, and probably not that long. The first vague impression that came to me was that I was being assisted to my feet, a man grasping my arm on my right and another on my left. Then, almost automatically, I began stumbling and walking, my wits clearing every moment until the whole truth dawned upon me.

Despite my care, an Apache warrior had stolen upon me from the rear, without detection. He had struck me a stunning blow as he leaped upon my shoulders and bore me to earth, where his comrade deprived me of my pistol. The stinging, ringing pain in my head told me that the blow, which brought me down, was a fierce one.

What impressed me as beyond explanation was that these two dusky demons had failed to kill instead of taking me prisoner. In that campaign against Geronimo and his band, it was not the custom on either side to take prisoners. This was especially true of the Apaches. They delighted too much in torture, outrage and suffering to let any opportunity for such dreadful work pass.

When I became certain that only two captors were with me, I resolved to seize the first opportunity and make a fight for it. I would pretend a weakness greater than was the fact, and then snatch out my sword and at them. I knew, of course, they had taken my pistol, but I could get on without that— the blade was sufficient.

The ground was rough, sometimes up, sometimes down, and again we circled boulders and rocks, and the stones and dirt crumpled under our feet. I had not walked far, under the uncertain light of the moon, when I discovered that my sword was gone. The scabbard would have flapped against my thigh or made itself felt in some way. Thus, I had no weapon of any kind with which to defend myself, while of course my captors were more fully armed than usual.

The two held a viselike grip on my arms, and evidently were prepared for any outbreak on my part. Moreover, though I am of the average height, each was fully as tall as I was. The Apache is generally of squat figure, and these, therefore, were of more than the usual stature. Having been smart enough to make prisoner an armed officer, they were not the ones to give him a hope of escape.

With my racking brain clear, I was certain that one of two things was intended. These bucks were taking me far enough away to indulge their fiendish will without fear of molestation, or they were conducting me to their camp that others might have part in the exquisite enjoyment. And yet I was wrong in both surmises.

Once or twice, the impulse was strong upon me to call for help. Some of our scouts must be in the neighborhood and would be quick to respond, but I was held silent by the manifest fact that, quick as they were, they could not be quick enough to save me. My captors would never allow me to be retaken. Accordingly, I held my peace, and partly stumbling, partly walking, and in anything but a calm frame of mind, I plunged farther among the hills that were the scene of so many stirring events that evening.

The bucks did not speak a word, for there was no occasion to do so. Nor did I indulge in any observations; for neither was there call in my case. It was an extraordinary promenade through that wild region on that still summer night.

The singular journey ended sooner than I expected. After clambering around a score of boulders, ascending and descending several steep slopes, I noticed that we were going through a narrow cañon-like passage in the mountains. This was followed for less than two hundred yards, when an abrupt change was made, and an instant later, I was among a group of more than twenty Apache warriors. No campfire was burning, but enough moonlight penetrated the gorge to give me glimpses of several faces. The first I recognized was Geronimo himself. The others were strangers. There was a good deal of talking in low tones, during which little attention was paid to me. It was useless to pretend weakness, and I was allowed to stand somewhat apart from the red men. I folded my arms, and contemplating the strange scene, asked myself what the end was to be.

To me only one end was possible. They were merely consulting as to the most pleasing method, to them, of torturing me to death. It would not take them long to agree, but again I was mistaken. Nothing of the kind was in their minds.

It was beyond my comprehension that this company of warriors, under the leadership of Geronimo, should halt for anything of that nature. I could conjure up no reason for such an unprecedented course, and in truth, there was none.

The council had lasted but a brief while, when one of the number came toward me, and pausing a step or two distant, addressed me in excellent English:

"My friend, you are doubtless astonished that in the circumstances you should be taken prisoner by these Apaches. I can make all clear in a few words. Your people have made captive of one of our most beloved chiefs, Martaña. We have made you prisoner in order that we can bring about an exchange. Several of our scouts have been out looking for a chance to secure one of your men, and it is your fate to fall into our hands. But you need not be alarmed. No doubt your commanding officer will be most happy to do his part, and I assure you that there shall be no lack of faith on our side."

What was my reply to these astounding words? Instead of speaking, I made the Masonic signal of distress, for I had recognized the man before me as Jared J. Jennings, whose Indian name was El-tin-wa, and whom I had first met some months before in my own lodge in the East.

He was attired in the same frowsy costume as the untidy Apaches around him, even to the bare head. His face was not painted, but his long, curling locks dangled about his shoulders. I should have recognized his voice, which was unusually musical, without the sight of his countenance. When he observed my appeal, he smiled.

"That is unnecessary, Brother Chichester," he said, "For I identified you before you did me, though I was unaware that you were with Lieutenant Smith until a brief while ago. Be assured that I can never forget my duty to a brother Mason. I need not add that were there no member of our tribe with you, I should have done all I could for you, at the risk of my life."

"I don't doubt that," was my grateful reply. "I am at your disposal."

I would have given much for an explanation from this remarkable man, but it was not mine to question him. I supposed he had returned to the Chippewas, among whom, as he told me, he had lived for a number of years. The last place where I expected to meet him was in the band of Warm Spring Indians, led by Geronimo, but here he was and evidently in high favor.

"You have no doubt of the willingness of Lieutenant Smith to agree to the exchange?"

"There can be none. How will it be managed? You know that no dependence can be placed on the word of an Apache."

"No more than upon the word of *some* white men; but," he added, sinking his voice, "some of these people, including Geronimo, understand English."

I accepted the valuable hint, and guarded my words uttered in the hearing of the party who were grouped around.

"How will the exchange be managed? Under a flag of truce?"

"Only metaphorically so. I will go with you to your camp and leave you to state the conditions of the exchange; you will stay and Martaña will accompany me back. Could anything be more simple?"

"Your plan is simplicity itself. When shall the start be made?"

"Now, for it is past low twelve, or as soon as I have had a little explanation with Geronimo." He turned and began talking with the chief in his native tongue. It was plain to me that the grim old fellow was dissatisfied. He preferred that Martaña should join him first. In that case, it is not likely I should have lived ten minutes after the return of the sub-chief, for Geronimo's ideas of honor were much the same as that of the majority of his race. Even El-tin-wa, with his undoubted "pull," would not be able to save me.

He talked long and earnestly with the leader, and finally prevailed. I do not know, and he never told me, what was said, but I am morally sure that Jennings staked his own life on the success of the plan he had formulated.

"He agrees to it," he said in his pleasant voice, "and since he is liable to change his mind, we will not delay; come with me."

And, turning my back upon that group of bloody miscreants, I walked as calmly up the ravine as if leaving a party of friends. I noticed that Jennings kept just behind me, as if to interpose his body as a shield. We had hardly turned the corner of the passage when he said in a low voice:

"Let us climb out here; turn to the right; I guess it is safe for me to lead."

He placed himself in the advance, and climbed gracefully up the sloping side of the dry cañon. I had left my revolver and sword behind. I should have been glad to get them again, but it was not worthwhile for me to ask for their return. Jennings himself, as far as I could see, had no weapons with him.

The peculiar situation gave safety to us both. None of the Apache scouts was likely to make trouble, for they would identify Jennings as quickly as I would, while the reverse would be the case if any of our own people observed us. Impressed with this fact, my friend ventured to talk as we picked our way through the hills toward the camp of Lieutenant Smith.

"Jennings," said I in a guarded voice, "I ought to tell you that Martaña is badly, and perhaps mortally, wounded."

"I am glad you did not say so where others could have overheard you. Geronimo knows that he is in your hands and that he must have been hurt, else he wouldn't have been captured, but he has no idea that it is as bad as you say."

"Suppose the chief dies before we reach camp?"

"That shall make no difference so far as *I* am concerned. I can think of no possible cause that will prevent your speedy joining of your friends. We have not far to walk, and we shall get there before the news can reach our camp."

The situation being such that neither of us was in personal peril, my companion talked freely. We had not gone far when, being slightly in advance, he abruptly stopped.

"Did you hear anything?" he asked in a low voice.

"No."

"Some one is hovering near us. It may be one of your scouts or one of ours; whoever it is makes no difference. Brother Chichester, how was it you fell into our hands?"

I briefly related the circumstances.

"No bravery or caution could prevent such a misfortune,

especially as the ones who captured you were out for the purpose of doing that sort of thing."

"I am sure, too, Brother Jennings, that we have a traitor in our camp."

"What camp is not thus afflicted?" was his non-committal response.

We were still facing each other, and I determined to press the question that had caused Lieutenant Smith and me so much mental disturbance. He opened the way.

"Do you know who your traitor is?"

"I received proof to-night that cannot be questioned."

"May I ask who he is?"

I saw no reason why I should withhold the information.

"Vikka, the most skilful scout with us."

At this moment, the moonlight fell full upon the face of my friend, and I noted his doubting smile. He slowly shook his head.

"You are mistaken."

I flushed indignantly at this attempt to screen a miscreant.

"You forget that I have had the proof."

"What was that proof?"

"I saw him and Geronimo in confidential converse hardly two hours ago."

"Will you be good enough to give me the particulars?"

I did so. Clearly, he was astonished that I should have remained crouching so near without being discovered by either.

"Did you hear what was said by them?"

"No; and had I been able to do so, I should not have understood a word."

"You say that Vikka held his blanket so far up about his shoulders that you could not see his face until he turned away after the chief had left?"

"Such was his action."

"Can you explain *why* Vikka should take such pains to conceal his countenance?"

"Only on the supposition that he feared some of his companions might be near, to whom his identity otherwise would have become known."

"If that were the fact, he would not have been so quick to reveal it to you when he turned to go away. That was not the case. The reason for his peculiar action was that he did not wish Geronimo to recognize him. He kept his face covered and spoke in low tones and, so far as he was able, in a disguised voice. His aim was to make the chief think he was *some other person*—the one who had served him before."

"You mean that he took the place of the real traitor and fooled Geronimo?"

"Not quite. Rather, he tried to do that, but failed, though he did not suspect it. Geronimo penetrated the deception, but kept the fact from Vikka, who never suspected that his trick had been read."

"How, then, do you explain the fact that through Vikka your leader learned the truth, for when we rushed your camp soon after all your people had fled?"

The man was still smiling as he made answer:

"Vikka assured him that your troopers were several miles distant. Knowing who said these words, Geronimo saw he was lying, and that the opposite was the fact; he acted upon this information. I have given you the truth."

"We have a traitor among us for all that, and your leader may have learned the real situation through him."

"No; he has been unable to hold any communication with the man for two days. He was on the lookout for him when Vikka appeared with his attempt at personating the other fellow."

"Who is this fellow?"

"Surely you cannot expect me to name him. I am a friend of the Apaches, and it would be base dishonor for me to betray our ally. I cannot permit you, however, to be unjust to a faithful scout. Vikka is unapproachable from our side. I know that of my own personal knowledge."

It gave me immeasurable relief to receive this assurance. I could not refuse to accept his explanation. A gross injustice had been done Vikka, and I longed for the chance to reassure Lieutenant Smith.

But who was the traitor? Despite the value of the minutes and the prudence of our getting back to camp immediately, I racked my brain in the effort to solve the torturing problem. I hastily ran over the names of the different scouts. The only one upon whom I could hang a suspicion was Chato, the cousin of Geronimo, but he was not with us just then, and I reflected, too, that none of us knew anything positive against him. It was his relationship to the Warm Spring leader that caused distrust.

"Well," said I with a sigh, "this business is costing both sides dear. You have lost some of your best men and so have we. One of our finest scouts was killed to-night, besides several who were hurt."

"Who of your scouts has fallen?"

"Pedro, the equal almost of Vikka. I never saw a braver fellow. He faltered before no danger."

I noted the start of Jennings. He was resting easily on one foot, but straightened up and asked in an excited undertone:

"Are you sure Pedro is dead?"

"There is no question about it; I saw his body."

"You have loosed my lips; now that the scout is no more, I will tell you that *he* was the friend of ours who served us best by staying in your camp; it was his place that Vikka attempted to take; he believes he succeeded in deceiving Geronimo, when it was Geronimo who deceived him."

"It looks, then, as if Vikka knew of the treachery of Pedro."

"There can be no question of that. If any proof were asked, it was given by the violent death of Pedro."

"You don't mean to say that Vikka—"

"Certainly; it was Vikka who drove his knife into his breast, as soon as he got the chance, after he learned the truth."

"But how did he learn the truth?"

"Of that I cannot be certain, but my belief is that when Geronimo first met Vikka between the lines he did not suspect the deception. Probably he pronounced the name of Pedro and thus gave him away. Vikka must have known that something of that nature was afoot, and he is shrewd enough to distrust the right person."

It was on my tongue to ask a pointed question or two of a personal nature, the answer to which would have explained how it was that the man who had spent most of his life with the Chippewa Indians was now living hundreds of miles away from their hunting grounds among the unspeakable Apaches; but I was hardly justified in probing the matter.

"I think we have been scrutinized sufficiently," quietly added my guide, "and now we will return to your camp, which is close at hand."

VI

LIEUTENANT SMITH had become much disturbed over my absence, and it was a vast relief to him when I walked into camp with my companion, whom I introduced with a statement of the business upon which he had come.

It was the first intimation that our commander had of the presence of a white man with Geronimo's band. His astonishment was great, but he was too much of a gentleman to express his feelings in the presence of the visitor. Being dressed like an Apache, it was easy to take Jennings for one, so long as he kept at a distance.

Most of the troopers and several of the scouts gathered round us three and listened with intense interest to our words. The racking headache, which had tormented me, was almost entirely gone, and naturally, I was in high spirits over the situation.

"It is the first time that we have exchanged prisoners with Geronimo," said the lieutenant, "but I shall be glad to keep up the custom, including other usages of honorable warfare."

"Thank you; nothing would please me more. You must make some allowance for uncivilized men who are pressed desperately hard. We have been a long time on our way here, and I shall be glad to accompany your prisoner back to our camp."

"And he will be equally glad, no doubt, to go with you; yonder he lies, apparently asleep, on that blanket, which I placed at his disposal."

It will be remembered that no fire was in the camp, a part of which was in shadow, though by this time, the moon was high in the sky, and when not hidden by clouds, a flood of light bathed the earth. A few paces beyond where we stood a dark, silent form was lying, as if the man felt no interest in what was going on around him.

Jennings walked over to him, stooped and touched his shoulder, saying something in Apache. There was no reply, and he bent lower. A moment followed and then he straightened up.

"Chief Martaña is dead!" he said with more excitement in his voice than I had ever heard.

"It can't be!" exclaimed Smith, as he and I hurried to his side.

Nonetheless, it was true. The poor fellow, stretched on the blanket, had quietly breathed out his life unnoticed by those around him. His body was still warm, and he had been dead but a short time.

"I cannot tell you how sorry I am, Mr. Jennings," said the lieutenant, who sincerely regretted the unfortunate occurrence.

"So am I," responded Jennings, "and yet no one is blamable for it. The most that can be said is that fate has given you the advantage."

The peculiar delicacy of the situation must have struck all three of us at the same moment. I had been sent into camp in exchange for Martaña, who was no longer among the living. Geronimo had performed his part of the bargain, originally proposed by him. It was out of our power to fulfill our part. What did honor require of me?

At first blush, it would seem that I should go back to the Apache camp with my conductor, thus restoring the situation to what it was at first.

But did equity demand the sacrifice? Were we dealing with a civilized enemy, there could be only one answer; but if I voluntarily placed myself in the power of the merciless

Apaches, it would be suicide on my part. Not an instant's mercy would be shown me.

Lieutenant Smith was the first to speak.

"I repeat, Mr. Jennings, that I am extremely sorry for this. You will report my words to Geronimo, and assure him that if at any time in the future one of his chiefs or warriors falls into our hands, he shall be immediately returned to him. That is the most I can say, for in no circumstances will I permit Lieutenant Chichester to go back to your camp."

"And I may add that if you gave such permission, I should refuse to take him with me to certain death."

"And if you will allow a word from me, no permission of the lieutenant or wish of Mr. Jennings would induce me to walk into the lion's den again. Therefore, *that* phase of the question is closed. That which now concerns me, Mr. Jennings, is how this is going to affect *you.*"

"What do you mean?" asked my friend.

"Will Geronimo accept your explanation? Will he not believe that we are retaining Martaña alive, or, if he is dead, that he was slain by us after capture?"

"I will attend to that," replied Jennings with a shrug of his massive shoulders. "Gentlemen, I bid you good-evening."

In addition, without another word he walked from the camp, while we gazed silently after him, hardly able for the moment to take in the whole situation. He must incur some risk from our scouts, some of whom were still out, and could not know of what had occurred, but he felt equal to the task, and I may as well say that he rejoined Geronimo without harm from our side.

As soon as I could get the opportunity, I told Lieutenant Smith what I had learned from Jennings concerning Vikka and Pedro. He was amazed.

"To think that neither of us suspected Pedro, but distrusted the faithful Vikka. Our only consolation is that he need never know of the shameful injustice we did him. Well, Pedro has met a deserved fate at the hands of our most loyal scout."

"I did not see Vikka among those in camp."

"He is out somewhere on duty. Lieutenant, while you have been fortunate in thus coming back, the Apaches have gained another important advantage over us."

"I do not understand."

"The singular situation that developed has checked our pursuit for a considerable interval. The hostiles have improved the chance and are making off in all haste."

"But they expected the wounded Martaña to join them."

"Two or three warriors have stayed behind to receive him, intending when he came up to place him on a horse and hurry after the main band. It is near morning, and we must lose no more time."

Even while he spoke a faint lighting up of the eastern sky showed. Soon the sun would touch the horizon and another hard day's work was before us.

"I should be glad to give Martaña a soldier's burial," said the officer, "but the best we can do is to treat him as we treat those scouts of ours who fall at the post of duty."

So the blanket was carefully gathered around the bronzed form as it lay flat on the earth, and thus it was left.

"Some of their scouts will probably visit our camp after we leave; if they have any doubt of the truth, they will be convinced by an examination of the body, unless," grimly added the officer, "they don't want to be convinced."

Before we started, Vikka and Jim came in, bringing the message that we anticipated. The main body of hostiles was well through the mountain spur and in the rough region beyond, pushing with all haste southward. It would take the hardest kind of riding to overtake them before nightfall. But we were determined to do it. Horses and men were refreshed from their rest and food, and we ought to cover a good many miles before the intolerable splendor of the summer day burst upon us.

At the moment of starting, Smith said:

"Lieutenant, I don't feel easy about that friend of yours. He is going to have a hard time to square matters with Geronimo. Do you think you can make your way back to the place where you left the Apaches?"

"I think so, but it will be better if I take one of our scouts with me."

"Choose your man."

"He is Vikka. I will tell him everything, excepting that either you or I ever distrusted him."

We left our ponies with the main body, which were to be guided over a trail well known to our scouts, while the veteran and I made our way by foot to the ravine down which I had been conducted some time before as a captive, to whom all prospect of escape was closed. Before we reached the most dangerous part of our venture, I compelled my companion to answer several questions. He had told me we were likely to come upon the Apaches who were waiting to receive Martaña, though they would not stay long after learning the truth.

I began by telling Vikka that I witnessed the meeting between him and Geronimo, being less than a dozen yards away from them during the interview. The fellow was astonished and could hardly believe it. I described the movement of each and told how he dropped his blanket from his face after the departure of the chief and when the scout had turned his back upon him. "That so—that so," he replied with a grin. We had stopped for the exchange of a few words, for the situation gave us the opportunity. With a smile that disclosed his gleaming white teeth, he asked:

"Why me put blanket over face?"

"You did that to prevent Geronimo seeing who you were."

"Me fool him—me what you say, 'shet up his eye.'"

"No, you didn't; he may not have known you by name, but he soon found out that you were not the fellow he was expecting."

"He call me 'Pedro'—he think me Pedro."

"He did so at first, but it took him only a minute to learn the truth."

"How you know dat?"

"That man who brought me into camp told me. Geronimo let you think you had fooled him, but you didn't. You told him our men were miles away."

"Yes, me tole him dat."

"But didn't you see from what followed that he didn't believe you? He knew you were not telling the truth and he broke camp in a hurry."

"Dat so," said my friend, as if communing with himself; "me think Pedro tole him, but dat could not be."

"Why not?"

"He did not get chance," was the significant response.

With no doubt as to how Pedro had been removed hence, I did not press the question that naturally rose in my mind.

When I had no thought of anything of the kind, the stiletto thrust came. Vikka gave an odd chuckle, and with a queer turn of his head said:

"You think me act like Pedro; Leften' Smith, he think so— think so some time."

I was frightfully embarrassed, but got out of it better than I deserved.

"It was a night of tragedy"

"Can't you imagine how I felt when I saw you talking to Geronimo, where you didn't believe any one else could know it? I *did* feel bad, Vikka."

"Leften' Smith—he not see me."

"But I told him about it."

"He think so *afore*—you think so *afore,* eh?"

"Well, we shall never doubt you again; even if I see you with your arm about the neck of Geronimo and your lips against his cheek, I shall know it is not you, but somebody else."

This brilliant witticism was satisfactory. Vikka might well claim he had the laugh on us, and I did not grudge him his triumph. We resumed our advance up the ravine, and, at his suggestion, I dropped behind until he could go forward and reconnoitre. It might be that some of our enemies were near, and it was impossible to be too careful.

The scout had not been absent from my sight ten minutes when I heard his guarded signal. It was a call for me to join him, and I did so. As I turned the bend in the gorge, he was standing upright on the spot where I had left the dozen hostiles when Brother Jennings started for our camp with me in charge.

Even before I reached him, I saw the form at his feet. It was a night of tragedy, and in the dim morning light, we had come upon another victim of atrocity. I identified the body as that of Jared J. Jennings.

He was lying on his side, as if in a calm slumber, but it was the slumber, which shall know no waking until the sounding of the last trump.

Vikka had read the whole sad story. So had I, and needed no enlightenment from him. The man had returned to Geronimo without the sub-chief whom he was to bring back in exchange for me and without me also. When an explanation was demanded, he told the truth. Martaña was dead, a fact which was not discovered until I was among my own people. Martaña had died on their hands without any blame on their part. I had refused to return with him, and the visitor could not compel me to do so. Lieutenant Smith had sent the pledge that if at any time one of Geronimo's warriors fell into the hands of the white men, he should be returned safely to the band. Thus, the exchange would be affected sooner or later, and the bargain carried out in spirit and letter.

Within the same minute that Jennings, or El-tin-wa, delivered this message, he died, stricken down by the hand of Geronimo himself. In his flaming rage, the remorseless chieftain believed that the white man had betrayed him for the purpose of befriending a stranger of his own race.

How did I learn these particulars? The main fact was self-evident when I looked down on what was left of the poor fellow who had really given his life for me. Nearly twenty years later, when Geronimo was an old man and a prisoner, I questioned him. He surlily refused to tell me anything, but I secured the help of Vikka, who was able to draw out the venerable scamp, and piecemeal he told the truth of one of the many atrocious crimes of which he had been guilty, though you will find no mention of it (nor of many others) in his biography lately published.

There was nothing that I could do for Brother Jennings. He lay as he had fallen, and, though his blood had dyed the ground, one arm was bent under the side of his head, as if he had lain down to peaceful slumber. Neither Vikka nor I had our blanket with us, or we should have wrapped him up in it; but we drew him to one side of the canon, carefully composed his stiffening limbs, and left him there.

As I looked down in that pale countenance, which I had

first seen in such different circumstances, I murmured:

"It is little that I know of you except that you gave your life for me, and greater than that no man can give. Would that it had been mine to thank you. Whatever fault you may have had, or whatever ill you may have done—and who of us has not gone astray?—surely it has been atoned for by this. *Requiescat in pace.*"

Regarding this remarkable man, who gave his name as Jared J. Jennings, and who was known among the Indians as El-tin-wa, I have consulted with many and set what investigations I could on foot. The theory which is the most reasonable, in my judgment, is that he went among the Chippewa Indians, as he claimed to have done, when quite young, that he married one of the tribe, and two children were born to the couple. The deaths of these and their mother were due to white men. It was impossible to know the circumstances, but the awful blow shadowed Jennings's life. Who could have had a more appalling grievance? In the hope of overcoming his intolerable resentment, he came east, mingled with his own race, and visited Masonic lodges, as he was entitled to do. Finally, his restlessness mastered him. He started suddenly for the Indian country, resolved to do all in his power to punish those who had wrecked his life.

It may have been that he had settled long before with the directly guilty, but if so, it did not suffice him. He forswore his race.

The Chippewas at that time, and indeed for a long time before, were on the best of terms with the whites, and he could not work out his terrible programme among them. Therefore, he made his way to the Southwest, where the Apaches were continually on the warpath, and cast in his lot with them.

Moreover, the spring of 1885 was not the first time he

went thither. He could not have become so familiar with their language and ways in that brief interval. Chato told me he had seen him with his people two years before his death, though Geronimo, when questioned, would never give any satisfactory reply.

I must not forget one peculiar fact, which involved the career of Jennings in still deeper mystery. It will be recalled that he said he was born in the city where I first sat in a lodge with him, that a sister had only recently died, and that his father had lived there for a good many years. An investigation, covering many months, failed to discover any traces of his relatives. That in one respect he told the truth I am convinced, but he deemed it best to hide his identity under an impenetrable veil by using a fictitious name for himself. At any rate, he is entitled to my grateful remembrance, and such he shall always have.

I need not pursue the subsequent history of that last campaign against Geronimo. No man who has not passed through a similar experience can comprehend the sufferings of those terrifying four months. The trail of the Apaches crossed and recrossed again and again, and led through mountains so wild that until then they had been deemed inaccessible to white men at least. With our forces strengthened, we kept at it. Scout Eduardy in one-week rode a single horse five hundred miles, and the distance, which we traversed, was equal to that between New York and San Francisco. The raiding and massacring covered a region four times as large as the State of Massachusetts, and during the campaign, three thousand soldiers were engaged on our side of the line and almost as many Mexicans south of the Rio Grande, who were as resolute as we to run the human wolves to earth.

Through a temperature like that of the infernal regions,

General Miles pressed his task. The heliograph flashed orders from one mountain peak to another, and General Lawton gave the hostiles no rest. Finally, worn out and exhausted, they halted near the town of Fronteras, in the Sierra Madre. There, while Geronimo was trying to make a treaty with the Mexicans, which would allow him to raid American territory, he was visited by Lieutenant Charles B. Gatewood, of the Sixth Cavalry, who spoke Apache and knew the desperate leader. In making this visit, that officer took his life in his hands, but by his tact, he convinced Geronimo that only one course was open to him. He took that course and surrendered.

So long as he was anywhere in the Southwest, however, none of the ranchmen felt safe. Consequently, he was removed eastward, far beyond the scene of his fearful crimes, and has been held there ever since. The last time I saw Geronimo was at the inauguration of President Roosevelt, on March 4, 1905. The old man, past four-score, with the tears streaming down his wrinkled cheeks, begged the President to allow him to return to his former home, for he must soon die. The President told him he had been so bad that he must wait a while longer, hinting at the same time that he was afraid that if Geronimo showed himself in some portions of the Southwest he would be killed by the incensed settlers, who could never forget his wicked deeds, and who would distrust him, even though he had passed far beyond the allotted age of man.

VII

AFTER TEN YEARS

ONE sultry afternoon in August, 1869, I was sitting in my parlor drowsily reading the daily paper, when I heard a quick step upon the porch, followed by the tinkling of the bell. Without waiting for the servant to answer, I stepped into the hall and drew the door open.

I saw standing before me a man in middle life, plainly but neatly dressed, of sandy complexion, smooth, pock-fretten face, pleasing expression and a striking brightness of manner.

"Good-afternoon, sir," he said, with a half-military salute; "are you Mr. Ellis, Master of Trenton Lodge, No. 5?"

I replied in the affirmative.

"Then I have to say that I am a Mason in distress and have come to you for help."

At that, I invited him to enter. Seating myself in front of him, I subjected him to a rigid examination; with the result that I found him one of the brightest Masons, I ever met. He could have presided over any lodge and conferred any and all of the degrees without the slightest hitch. Satisfied on this point, I asked him to tell his story.

"It is a long one," he replied with a smile, "but I think I can promise you it is interesting."

"I am sure of that," I said, settling back on a sofa, and placing a large chair at his disposal, "don't omit any particulars."

After Ten Years

Nearly two-score years have passed since I listened to one of the most remarkable stories I ever heard. I took no notes of what my visitor said, and it is quite possible that I may slip on a few minor points, such as names, but the narrative itself will remain with me as long as I live. I was impressed by the man's candor, his intelligence and his apparent truthfulness. I have never doubted a single thing he told me.

"My name is John Wilkins," he said, "and my home is, or rather was, in Knoxville, Tenn. Having told you that much, I must go back ten years before the breaking out of the Civil War. It was in 1851 that I was a passenger on a steamer going up the Mississippi to my home. I was in good circumstances, being the owner of a prosperous grocery, and was the father of two boys and a daughter. Several years previous I had suffered from small-pox, escaping death by a hair's breadth, but at the time I have in mind I was in superb health, with a natural flow of spirits, and, if I must confess it, not quite fully over a certain wildness of conduct at which I now wonder, though I cannot say that it ever involved me in serious trouble.

"One cold, drizzly afternoon the passengers on the steamer were thrown into a panic by the discovery that a man in one of the cabins had broken out with small-pox. A dozen of the most excited demanded of the captain that he should put the unfortunate fellow ashore and leave him to die in the woods.

"Being immune, I made a stealthy visit to the cabin of the sick man and discovered two important facts. He unquestionably had the disease, but he had had it for several days, and was convalescing. He might be considered out of danger, as far as he himself was concerned, but, as you know, the risk from contagion was as great, if not greater, than before.

"The second truth that came to me was the discovery that

the man was a Free Mason. I assured him he should be taken care of, and told him to give himself no anxiety on that score. Promising to come to him again in a short time, I slipped out of his cabin, without attracting notice, and made my way to the deck, where the captain was standing near the pilot house with a score of men, pale, swearing and more excited than ever. He was awed by the display of anger and deadly resolution on the part of the mob. I listened for several minutes before I could get the run of the talk. The men were demanding more fiercely than before that the boat should be turned to land. He was arguing and protesting, for his soul revolted at the unspeakable brutality of the thing, but he could not withstand them.

"'Oh, well,' he exclaimed with an impatient oath, 'you are a set of infernal fools; but since you insist on it, I'll do it.'

"I knew what he meant and my blood boiled.

"'You'll do *what?'* I shouted above the din and confusion.

"'Why, set this poor devil ashore and let him die alone in the woods,' replied the captain, purposely giving this extra twist, as may be said, to his rage.

"'By the Eternal!' I shouted, 'the first motion you make to do that I'll shoot you dead in your tracks!'

"I had my pistol in my hand and brandished it over my head. My words, looks and manner were for the moment like a bombshell. I backed off, weapon in hand and before the mob could recover and attack me, I shouted:

"'The sick man is a Free Mason! Brothers, rally to my support, for never was one of your brothers in sorer need of it.'

"Well, sir, you ought to have seen what followed. Other passengers were swarming on the upper deck, drawn by the magnet of a danger that threatened them all. There must have been nearly a hundred of them. On hearing my appeal,

, they began breaking apart, pushing away from one another and many of them grouping around me, until two parties, about equal in numbers, faced each other on the deck. I had stepped nearer the captain, and my new friends followed me. He was somewhat bewildered by the suddenness of everything, but he kept his head pretty well.

"I don't believe there was a man in either party who did not own a pistol or bowie knife, and not a few displayed both. There were pale, resolute faces among those merchants, planters, and gamblers, and they glared like tigers at my friends, the captain and me.

"'God! This is awful,' said the captain to me in a scared undertone.

"'Don't you fear,' I assured him; 'this is *our* fight; you have nothing to do with it; leave everything to us.'

"Now, I think I may take credit to myself for seizing the psychological moment for executing a coup. As sure as the sun shines, there would have been one of the bloodiest and most desperate fights ever known on the Mississippi within the next few minutes had I not faced the scowling mob and raised my hand.

"'Friends,' I called, 'there *is* a man in one of the cabins who has the small-pox, and the fact that he is getting well won't lessen your danger for several days. You have the right to protect yourselves against that hideous disease, and you can do it better than by dumping the poor fellow on the banks to die like a rabid dog. I have had the small-pox; I am not afraid of it; I will go into his room and nurse him; no one else need come near him; the servants can bring the food to a certain point safely removed from the cabin, and when they are gone I will come out and get the food; no medicine is needed, for the time for that has passed; the man will be completely isolated, and none of you will be in the slightest danger. What do you say?'

"Well, I had captured them. The crowd broke up, moving slowly here and there, all fraternizing, while some of those who had been the most insistent for the commission of the dreadful crime shook me by the hand and declared they never meant what they said. Nonetheless, they still would have insisted upon marooning the sick man had I changed my mind and refused to go into his cabin.

"The promise I made was faithfully carried out. The patient never knew from me of the scene on the upper deck, though I think it likely it reached his ears afterward from another source. I sat in his room for hours, reading and talking and doing all I could to cheer him. He really did not need anything of that nature, for the most exhilarating physical condition in which any person can be placed is that of convalescence. You get used to high health, but convalescence is new, thrillingly comforting and delightful, and by the time you become somewhat accustomed to it, its exquisite pleasure deepens and intensifies.

"I never saw a man improve more rapidly than my friend. Of course, we exchanged names, and before I finish you shall learn his. Neither of us had ever heard of the other, but that we became the warmest of comrades was inevitable. It is said that the one who does a kindness to another feels tenderer toward him than does the recipient toward the other. This man was an educated man of the highest honor and was filled with profound gratitude. He did not gush, but merely thanked me, adding:

"'I hope you will never be in trouble, but should such be your lot, you may command me to the death. *Remember that,*' he added with solemn significance.

"When we reached Louisville my friend was substantially

well, though the marks of his disease would show for a long time, and it was hardly prudent for him to venture out, except when absolutely necessary. My intention was to leave the steamer at that point, attend to some business matters in the interior, and to reach my home in Knoxville in the course of a couple of weeks; but I thought it best not to part company with the gentleman, who was too considerate to express the wish that I should stay by him any longer. His face lit up with pleasure when I quietly told him of my intention to see him through to his home.

"At Louisville we had to change steamers. The captain of the new boat was a Free Mason, and when I told my story to him, he promptly gave all the help needed. Arm in arm we two walked upon his boat at midnight and went to our cabin. No other person besides the captain had a suspicion of the truth.

"By the time we reached the landing where my friend was to leave the boat he was well, though the discolorations on his face, of course, were plain. I had accepted his invitation to go to his home with him. He wished me to make him an old-fashioned visit, but I assured him I could stay only one night. He would not consent to this until I promised to use the first chance to spend several weeks with him. It was my intention to do so, but somehow or other the opportunity never came.

"He was expected, and his Negro coachman was waiting for him. We were driven to one of the finest residences I have ever seen. He was a man of wealth, of culture, and of refinement, and was well known throughout the State. I never received kinder or more hospitable treatment than from him and his wife and daughter, of whom any husband and father might be proud. Late at night, when we sat alone in his drawing room, smoking and chatting, he suddenly asked:

"'And now how much do I owe you, Mr. Wilkins?'

"I took out a bit of paper and pencil and figured for a minute or two.

"'As nearly as I can make it, it is six dollars and fifty cents,' I replied; 'that is the extra fare for going somewhat out of my way.'

"He took his pipe from his mouth, smiled and shook his head.

"'That won't do.'

"'Why not? Can you make it any different?' I asked.

"'It is a hundred dollars at least. That will never repay you. Who would have done as much for me as you have done?'

"'You for me, are we not brother Masons?'

"He looked calmly in my face and smoked for a minute or two in silence. He saw I was in earnest, and without speaking, paid me my extra fare to and from Louisville. With the rare tact, which was natural to him, he made no further reference to my services.

"The next morning I bade him and his family good-by. Just as the coach was starting for the landing, his daughter hurried out of the door and placed a sealed letter in my hand.

"'Father says you are not to open that till you get home,' she said.

"I nodded and promised as I shoved it into my coat pocket. When I broke the seal a fortnight later, the first thing that caught my eye was a hundred dollar bill. Pencilled on a sheet of paper were the words:

"'If it should ever be in my power to do you any favor, no matter of what character, I beg that you give me the opportunity.'

"Bear in mind that all this took place in 1851. Ten years later came our great Civil War. You people in the North know nothing of what we suffered in the Border States, nor, indeed, do the people of the South itself, though they have had to drink the cup to its dregs. But in Knoxville, as in certain parts of Kentucky and Missouri, it was unadulterated hell, for the Secessionists and Unionists were about equally divided. It grew hotter and more frightful every day. In the same city, the same street, the same square, the same house, men met who were eager to spring at one another's throats and were only waiting for the chance to do so. I was a pronounced Union man from the start, and my two boys, one of whom was just old enough, enlisted in the Federal army. I stayed at home to look after my business or until the necessity for my leaving should become more urgent. After a time the Secessionists gained to a large extent, the upper hand. Parson Brownlow and a few of us used to meet secretly to discuss and decide upon the best course to follow, if, indeed, any course was open to us other than to bide our time.

"Some of the hotter-headed Unionists began burning bridges in different parts of the State with the purpose of harassing Confederate military movements. This continued after a number of them had been shot, and it was proclaimed that any one found guilty of the crime would be punished with death.

"Hardly a day passed that men were not arrested on the street charged with bridge burning and thrust into jail. One day, just as I came out of my house, I was taken in charge by two soldiers in command of a corporal and hustled off to jail. When I was thrust into the suffocating place, I found more than sixty of my friends and neighbors all charged with the same offence."

At this point in Wilkins's story, I interrupted him.

"See here, my friend, the war is over and you needn't be afraid to tell me the truth. *Did* you help burn any of those bridges?"

He chuckled.

"No; I was innocent, though if they had waited two nights longer I should have had to plead guilty in order to be honest. We had a big scheme on foot, but one of our number betrayed us. I know who he was, but will say nothing more, for he has been dead several years, and it is as well, also, that I do not refer to the manner of his taking off.

"If it be conceivable, matters grew worse. They kept bringing more prisoners and shoving them in upon us, until we hardly had room to move about. Finally, Parson Brownlow himself was fairly thrown into the big room with us. Well, he was a character. He could pray harder, sing louder and use more sulphurous language toward the Secessionists than any ten men north or south of Mason and Dixon's line. The style in which he denounced the Southern Confederacy and all the leaders in it, from the President down, made one's hair fairly rise on end. I can see him now, as the gaunt, spare preacher stood up among us, his eyes blazing, while he rolled out his denunciations and called down the vengeance of God upon the enemies of the Union. Then he would tell us of our duties to one another as well as to our country. I have seen the tears course down his cadaverous cheeks while thus pleading with us to lead pure and godly lives. Then all at once he would break out with his strong and not over musical voice into one of the sweet, grand old Methodist hymns, followed by a prayer, like that of some inspired prophet of old.

"One favorite expression of his was that we who suffered imprisonment or death for our principles were doing our country as much good and were as much martyrs for the Union as if we fell in battle. He drove that truth in upon us, seasoned with the assurance that those at whose hands we suffered should receive full punishment, not only in this world, but also in the life to come.

"We had been in prison only a few days when an orderly came to the door with a slip of paper in hand, and called out in a loud voice the names of two of the prisoners. They rose to their feet.

"'Come with me,' said the orderly; 'the provost-marshal wants you.'

"They followed him out of the door. A few minutes later, we heard the discharge of several guns, as if fired by a platoon. We looked at one another with scared faces. All knew what it meant; our two neighbors had been shot. Whether they had taken any part in bridge burning, I do not know. Evidently, there had been a secret investigation, and they had been pronounced guilty.

"Precisely the same thing took place the next day and the day following that. Since no one could shut his eyes to the fearful truth, it was the custom in each instance for Parson Brownlow to offer up a prayer, denounce the Confederate authorities in his red-hot fashion, while the victims shook the hands of all in turn. Then they went out and met their fate like heroes.

"We prisoners received visitors now and then; our jailers making no objection, for no harm could follow from such calls. I remember a mild old Quaker who came every day. He spoke kindly to all of us, sometimes bringing us delicacies or messages from our families and friends, and bearing away such messages, as we had to send. His visits were the only rays of sunshine that pierced the woeful gloom, and he was feelingly thanked over and over again for this thoughtfulness.

"One day I pencilled the following words on a small piece of paper and handed it to him:

"'The man who befriended you ten years ago when you were taken down with small-pox on a Mississippi steamer is now in Knoxville jail unjustly charged with bridge burning.'

"'Will you be kind enough to mail that for me?' I asked, handing the paper to him. 'Read it first.'

"He deliberately adjusted his spectacles, held the slip at arm's length and carefully read the line or two.

"'I don't know,' he replied; 'these are troublous times, my friend; those few words may mean more than they seem to mean. The authorities allow me to visit thee and thy friends on the understanding that I am to take no unfair advantage of the opportunity.'

"'I give you my word of honor,' I said, 'that the words have no other meaning than what they show on their surface.'

"He hesitated for a moment or two and then crumpled up the paper and shoved it into his waistcoat pocket, with the remark:

"'I cannot make thee any promise, but I will see what I can do.'

"The summary executions went on as before, with the same horrible detail—the calling out in a loud voice of two names, the farewell and shaking of hands, Parson Brownlow's prayer, with a few words of exhortation and the promise to look after the families of the victims, so far as it should be possible to do so, and then a few minutes after the doomed ones had passed out the whole company burst into singing 'The Star Spangled Banner.' One object of this was to drown the sound of the volley, which we knew would soon be fired. We became so accustomed to the report that we knew just when to expect it; but sing as loud as we might, we never failed to hear the awful crash, which pierced the walls of the jail.

"You cannot imagine the breathless hush which came over us when the door opened and we caught sight of the orderly with the little slip of paper in his hand. When the names were pronounced, the scene which I have described invariably followed. It is said that men can become accustomed to anything, but that tomb-like pause as we concentrated all our faculties upon the dread form as he was about to pronounce the doom of two of our number never lost its deadly intensity. There was always a moment or two when I do not believe a man in the room breathed.

"One dismal, drizzly morning, when we were all shivering with cold, the messenger of fate seemed to shout with more fiendish loudness than ever before.

"'William R. Jones and John Wilkins!'

"When the solemn hush ended we began shaking the hands of those who crowded around us.

"'Well, boys,' said I with a mirthless smile, 'my turn has come. Good-by!'

"'Remember,' fairly shouted the parson, 'you are dying as much for your country as did your comrades at Manassas and before Richmond. This can't go on much longer; these hell-hounds will soon run their race and God will smite them in His wrath.'

"It seemed to me that the parson put more unction into his prayer than usual, while the scowling orderly stood at the door and impatiently awaited the close of the exercises. As I finally passed out, I heard the strains of our national song, sung with a heartiness and vigor that thrilled me through.

"The orderly walked in the direction of the provost marshal's office, with me just behind him and my neighbor at my heels. The provost was a large man, whom I had known for years as possessing a furious temper. He was very profane and one of the fiercest Secessionists in the State. When I entered his office, he was savagely smoking a huge cigar, the smoke of which partly obscured his flaming features. Glaring at me as I halted near the door and looked at him seated in front of his desk, he fairly shouted with a sulphurous oath:

"'I should like to know what *that* means!'

"He held in his hand, which shook with anger, a yellow piece of paper that I saw was a telegram. The writing on it was so large that I read the words from where I was standing:

"'WAR DEPARTMENT, Richmond, Va.
"'.....................Provost-Marshal, Knoxville, Tenn.:

"'Release John Wilkins from custody at once and do not allow him to be molested or disturbed in person or property. Allow him to pass back and forth between the Confederate and Federal lines without question.

"'By order of
"'JAMES A. SEDDON,
"'Secretary of War, C. S. A.'

"James A. Seddon was the gentleman whom I had befriended in time of sore need, and it was to him my few pencilled lines were addressed which I handed to the Quaker visitor at our jail. He had mailed them to Richmond, and it had no sooner been read by Secretary Seddon than he telegraphed the order for my release.

"A glance at the writing and the whole truth flashed upon me. I could not conceal my exaltation of spirits, and as the provost marshal still held the telegram at arm's length, as if it were a venomous serpent, he took his cigar from his mouth and again roared with a number of oaths:

"'I say, what does *that* mean?'

"I should like to know what *that* means!"

"'Since it is written plainly enough for me to read it from where I stand, I should think you ought to be able to do so.'

"He glared at me as if about to burst with rage, swung around in his chair with a snort of disgust, and waved the orderly away with me. He had probably given his orders to the man and was unable to do justice to the situation. On the outside I was told I was at liberty to go whither I chose.

"General Burnside at that time was besieging Knoxville and drew the cordon close. Taking advantage of my strange permission, I passed into his lines, where, being well known to a number, I was well received. I made the trip back and forth several times, doing considerable in the way of trade. It was rare that any one was given such privileges as I, and the situation was not only peculiar, but also so dangerous that it could not last. For a civilian to pass freely from the lines of one army to those of their enemy, when he was known to be the foe of one, was an anomaly in warfare that must soon terminate.

"When the curious condition had lasted something over a week I was fired upon one night when turning a corner of the street in Knoxville. The man who discharged the pistol was not more than a dozen feet distant. I saw the flash and I heard the whistle of the bullet in front of my eyes. Instead of breaking into a run, he coolly walked off as if he did not care a rap whether I identified him or not. It would have been useless for me to demand his punishment or to appeal for protection. I knew I was certain to be shot if I remained, and the man who did me up would never suffer therefrom. Therefore, the next time I went into Burnside's lines I stayed there. My two sons were serving under him, and I was given employment in the commissary department, in which I remained to the close of the war.

"When it was safe for me to visit Knoxville again, I found

that my property had utterly vanished, and I was not worth a dollar beyond the pay I had saved. My wife had died at the outbreak of the war and both my sons had been killed in battle. My only daughter married about that time and moved with her husband to the North. Like thousands of others in the South, it was necessary for me when fifty years old to begin life over again.

"I had enough from my pay to take me to Canada, where I made my way to a lumber camp and hired out as a day laborer. My companions were good-hearted and kind, though rough, rugged and strong as bears. They forgot sometimes that I was not as tough as they were, and the work, which I undertook, was often beyond my power. I strove to the utmost to 'hold up my end,' anxious not to betray my physical weakness.

"One day while straining to lift a large piece of timber I felt something give way within me, and seized with a sudden deathly nausea, I sank to the ground in a faint. When I rallied, I was so weak that one of the men had to help me to the cabin in which we slept and ate our meals. There I was put in my bunk and a messenger brought a country doctor from the nearest village, which was a dozen miles away. The physician did all he could for me, but he had not the remotest idea of what was the trouble. He left me some simple medicines and promised to come again in the course of two or three days.

"Well, I lay in my rough bed for six weeks, during which time there was not a single movement of my bowels. The lower part of my body seemed as inert as so much wood. The doctor was not able to give me the slightest help, but always left me some of his medicine, which I religiously took according to instruction. I was too weak to leave my bed for more than a minute or two, and seemed to get neither better nor worse. Injections and every means possible were tried and produced not the slightest effect.

"As I said, six weeks passed away without any change in my condition. As I lay awake one afternoon, it occurred to me that it was time to take some of the medicine, which was on a rough stand beside my bed. I rolled over on one side and reached out my hand for the phial. At that instant, I thought a cannon had been discharged in the cabin. I lunged head foremost and tumbled upon the floor, where I lay like a dead man until some of my friends came in to prepare supper, and lifted me upon the couch again.

"Then the truth was discovered. A rupture of the bowels had taken place on my left side, and through the opening thus formed passed all the food that I ate, with the exception of a small proportion, which sometimes found its way into the bladder. The relief that had thus come gave me strength enough to walk, and by and by, I felt so well that no one would suspect that anything was the matter with me. It was utterly impossible, however, for me to do any kind of manual labor. I made my way to the hospital in Montreal, where after a time I was discharged as incurable. I journeyed to Philadelphia, where I went through the same experience. I am now on my way to my married daughter in Troy, where I expect to end my days. Being without a dollar to my name, I am compelled to apply to my Masonic brethren for assistance."

Mr. Wilkins told me that the only food he dare eat was mush and milk. I gave him a meal of that, and saw the opening in his side, over which he carried a bandage, something like a truss. I handed him, in the name of my lodge, more money than he asked for, shook his hand, and still smiling and with his farewell accompanied by a bright jest, he passed out of my home and I never saw or heard of him again.

VIII

CAMPING ON HIS TRAIL

(It is proper to state that in the following sketch the names of the places and persons for good reasons are fictitious. "Jerry Chattin," who related the incidents to me, is a prominent Free Mason, no doubt well known to many of my readers.)

I ONCE firmly believed that Jim McGibbon and I were ordained to be the bitterest of enemies, and it did seem to me that everything joined to increase the intensity of hatred which began in boyhood. Jim was about my age and lived at the small town of Champlain, in southwestern Missouri, while my home was at Verneau, some twenty miles away.

We first clashed as the captains of rival baseball clubs. Nowhere in the world is the struggle in our national game so determined and often so unfair as between near-by towns and villages. Nothing in the professional world can compare with it. The championship struggle between Champlain and Verneau was as bitter as bitter could be. One season we secured the coveted honor and the next year it went to our rivals. More than once the strife became a veritable battle, in which the inoffensive umpire, who strove to be just, was mobbed and would have suffered grave injury but for the rally of the club whom he was accused of favoring to his defence. Several times the games broke up in rows, in which the spectators were involved. It was shameful, but I am grieved to say that the same disgraceful scenes are still seen in other parts of the country.

It was natural in the circumstances that Jim and I should collide. Strict truth compels me to admit that in these bouts I generally got the worst of it, for Jim was taller, more active and a better boxer than I. Without giving any of the particulars, the last season, which saw the struggle for the championship, ended in a tie. I cannot help believing that this was the result of an unfair decision on the part of the umpire against us, but since such is the invariable explanation, I shall let it go at that.

In the autumn of 1860, Jim and I were sent east to college. As proof of our mutual dislike, I may say that after I had matriculated at Princeton, Jim, who appeared at the same place two days later with a similar purpose, deliberately insulted me by the remark:

"I have lived too long in the same State with you; New Jersey isn't big enough for both of us. I'd rather go to Tophet than abide in any college with the like of you."

With which he deliberately packed his trunk and went off to New Haven, without waiting for me to get back a suitable reply, which I did not think of until he was aboard of the cars on the way to the Junction, there to board the New York train and to go farther eastward.

We had each been in college a year when the great Civil War came. It was not long before I saw that Missouri was sure to become one of the most harried States in the Union. Nowhere was the strife as merciless and vicious as in the Border States, where hundreds of families were broken up by the fratricidal struggle.

I was not sorry when my father sent for me to leave college, but I was pained to learn upon arriving home that the general disarrangement of business had brought a reverse to him which made it impossible to keep me longer at Princeton. He, like myself, was strongly Union in his sentiments, and neither he nor my mother nor my sister made any objection when I announced my purpose of enlisting under the old flag, whose supporters in that part of the country at first were at great disadvantage. It seemed to me that the Secessionists were more numerous and more resolute, and for a time they had the upper hand. You know they came within an ace of burning the city of St. Louis, and we could make little headway against Sterling Price, and the governor and authorities who were back of him.

I was with Colonel Mulligan in his desperate but hopeless battle against Price at Lexington, and was taken prisoner, but soon afterward exchanged. It was at that time that I learned Jim McGibbon was a lieutenant under Price. I suspect that if he had discovered I was serving on his side, he would have joined the Union forces. I saw him but once during my captivity, and each sneered at the other without speaking. The situation was one of those to which words could not do justice.

Well, six months later I was at the head of a troop of irregular cavalry raiding through southwestern Missouri. I had two-score men under me, and they were as brave fellows as ever rode in saddle. There was hardly a man among them who was not inspired by one or more personal grievances. One had had a brother shot after surrender, another's home had been laid in ashes, others had suffered in some way, and they were not the men to let any chances at reprisals pass unimproved. Truth compels me to say that the outrages perpetrated by us were as much outside the pale of civilized warfare as were those of our enemies. It is a sad, sad story upon which I do not wish to dwell. How many memories linger with our gray-headed men of that bitter strife which they would fain forget! If, according to General Sherman, war is hell, civil war is hell-fire and damnation.

From reports that reached me, McGibbon was also in command of a squad of irregular cavalry that was about the equal in numbers to my company. There was no questioning his personal courage, and he was as anxious to meet me, as I was to meet him. A number in both commands were old acquaintances, and half of my fellows would have given their right hands for the chance of a set-to with his raiders. They were as fierce and at times as merciless as—well, as ourselves.

Now a situation came about, or, rather, several situations, which I have never been able to explain. For weeks and months, McGibbon and I raided through southwestern Missouri, over an area several hundred miles in extent, with the yearning prayer on the part of each for a fair stand-up fight between our companies. I was searching for him and he was hunting just as assiduously for me, and yet it looked as if fate had ordained we should never meet. More than once, we missed each other by less than an hour. I was hot on his trail one autumn day, and had actually caught sight of his horsemen as they raised a hill less than a mile away, when another body of cavalry, larger than both of us together, and all red-hot Secessionists, debouched on the scene and we had to gallop for our lives.

On another occasion, I broke camp just north of the town of Jasonville, and rode off at a leisurely pace to the eastward. Unsuspected on my part, McGibbon and his men dashed into the camp I had left, and came after us like so many thunderbolts. I did not learn the fact until a week later, and then heard that he, too, was turned off almost in the same manner that I had been diverted from my game. We managed to send exasperating messages to each other, in which there were mutual charges of cowardice accompanied by red-hot challenges. As I said, how we failed to meet in the circumstances is and has always been beyond my comprehension.

One dismal, drizzly day in October, finding myself within a short distance of Verneau, I decided to ride into the town and call on my folks. The place contained about a thousand inhabitants, almost equally divided in sentiment. We cared nothing for that, since nearly all the able-bodied men were absent fighting on one side or the other.

While still some distance from the town, I was disturbed to observe smoke rising in heavy volumes. We spurred our horses into a gallop, and had not yet reached the outskirts when what I dreaded proved true. Three dwelling houses were in flames, and among them was the home in which I was born and which was all that was left of my father's former wealth. The other dwellings were those of prominent Unionists, and in each case, a young man of my command was a member of the suffering household. Although most of those who had been spared were disunion in principles, they were good neighbors and gave shelter to all who had been so cruelly robbed of their homes.

I found father, mother and my sister with one of these families, without whose kindness it would have gone hard with them, for the raiders who had done this savage thing would not allow their victims to save the most insignificant part of their furniture or effects.

It proved as I suspected. Jim McGibbon and his band had made a flying visit to Verneau, looted a number of houses, and burned the three that we found in ruins. He was especially exultant over my parents and sister.

"Tell that coward son of yours," he said to my father, "that I've been looking a long time for him, but he always skulks out of my way. Do not forget to let him know that it was I, Jim McGibbon, who put the torch to this shack, and that if he wants to settle with me, he knows where to look. He's the chump I'm after."

"Did he say where he could be found?" I asked, pale faced and doing my utmost to restrain my rage.

"He said something," replied my father, "but in the confusion and excitement of the moment I did not catch the words, and if I did, have forgotten them."

I appealed to mother and sister, but they professed equal ignorance. Good souls, each one knew where the miscreant was waiting, but purposely kept the knowledge from me. They understood too well, what would follow, and they shuddered at the thought of a meeting between us.

The houses, which had been burned, stood so apart from the others that there was no danger of the flames communicating with those toward whose owners the guerrillas were friendly. McGibbon was careful in that respect.

When I found that nothing was to be gained from my people, I formed a resolution, which I took care to keep from them. I did not wish to have them beg and plead with me, and therefore gave no hint of what was in my mind. I whispered it to several of my comrades, and they eagerly agreed with me.

I stayed in the town for an hour or so, and the communion with my people would have been sweet but for what I had seen and learned. It was my custom, when my duties allowed, making these hurried, stolen visits, though they were always accompanied by great danger. There was more than one person in Verneau who would have been glad to betray me to my enemies, and I know that in several cases the attempt was made. Consequently, upon leaving my men encamped at some distance, I had to use extreme care to avoid the traps that were set for me. Of course, it was different when I took my men along. We were able to look out for ourselves, and would have welcomed a brush.

Up to this time, there had been something in the nature of neutrality between McGibbon and me concerning our own homes. I had kept away from Champlain and he had not molested Verneau. Each could find plenty to do elsewhere. But my enemy had broken this truce, and I determined to strike back. Consequently, after riding a short way from town, the troop turned their horses toward Champlain, and we arrived there late in the afternoon.

I knew where the home of McGibbon stood. Striking the heavy knocker on the door, I told his crippled father, who answered the summons, what his son had done and that I had come to retaliate. Jim had no brothers or sisters, but only his aged parents. What pity I might have felt for them in other circumstances was destroyed by the bitter memories of what he had done to my people. The couple was so mild and gentle, and refrained so carefully from protests and appeals, that I could not help feeling a pang or two, after all, when, after they had found refuge elsewhere, I applied the torch to their dwelling with my own hand. Two other buildings were fired by my men, and then we considered the accounts balanced.

We had all cherished the hope that when McGibbon found himself so near his own home he would pay it a visit, and the fight for which we both longed would come off, but he had not been there, and I had no more idea of where to look for him than if we had been dropped into the middle of the Atlantic.

"You will doubtless see your son before long," I said to his father, as I sat in the saddle with my horse reined up in front of his new quarters. "Don't forget to let him know that I, Jerry Chatten, did this because he burned my own home. He began the game and he will find I can play at it as well as him. I'm only sorry that he isn't here himself, but we shall meet before long."

The good man stood at the gate, gazing up in my face, which was illumined by the glare from his own burning home. I can never forget the picture, for he held his battered hat in his hand, looking for all the world like a patriarch of old. He had no words of reproach to utter, nor did he seem to feel the slightest ill will toward me. I even fancied I saw a mournful smile upon his beneficent countenance as he said in a voice as gentle as that of a woman:

"I am sorry, Jeremiah, that you and James are not friends. I hope you will become so before either of you passes away. I shall pray that it may be thus."

What a strange farewell from one whose home I had just destroyed! It made me feel queer all over, and I muttered as I rode off in the gathering gloom:

"How can *such* a father have *such* a son?"

Lieutenant Marsden, riding at my side, had a habit of speaking his mind. Discipline in that respect was never very strict in our company.

"I wonder now, cap, whether McGibbon isn't thinking the same about *you.*"

"It may be," I growled; "none the less, I'd give anything in the world to meet him."

"So would I; don't forget that he burned *my* folks out of house and home."

Since McGibbon had left definite word with my parents where I could find him and his band and I did not go there, he had good reason to proclaim that I was afraid of him. He had given the information only to my people, so it was useless for me to apply elsewhere. I could not blame my friends for their silence, but all the same, it roiled me.

A week went by, during which I was unable to get any trace of my enemy. He seemed to be raiding in the neighborhood, and I did my share, but the same unaccountable perverse fate kept us apart, when, as I have said, each was straining every nerve to get at the other.

The peculiar conditions of this local civil war compelled the combatants to rely to a great degree upon surreptitious information. It may be said that there was not a village, however small, in a large part of Missouri, which did not hold a number of Secessionists and Unionists. It was risky for them to give out information, but they gave it, and some of them paid the penalty with their lives.

One day word upon which I relied came to me that McGibbon and his company were to spend that night with friends in Jasonville, only eight or ten miles away. Most of the people there were disunionists, and it was not to be expected that he intended any kind of raid. He would probably go thither for a night or two for rest, for his men had been so continuously in the saddle that they needed it, as our own fellows often did.

I quickly formed my plan. As soon as it was dark, we would ride to within a mile or so of the town and take our position in a dense wood, with which we were all familiar. Then late at night, we would make a dash into the town and set things humming. Perhaps the long hoped-for meeting between McGibbon and me would follow. At any rate, we should be able to strike a blow that would tell.

In a situation like the one I have described the utmost care was necessary. It might be that my informant was mistaken. It might happen, also, that with all the circumspection I could use, McGibbon would get wind of what was afoot and would turn the tables on us. Matters could not have been more critically delicate. The wood to which I have alluded extended for several miles, almost to the edge of the town. If

McGibbon should learn of my coming, it would be the easiest thing in the world for him to form an ambuscade and empty half of my saddles at the first fire.

Because of this fact, I halted my men a mile out, and rode forward alone until close to the town, when I dismounted and tied my horse in the shadow of the trees, for the night was a bright, moonlight one. I was doing a risky thing, for I was taking the chances which I would not permit my men to run, but I relied upon the partial disguise of my slouch hat and the fact that forty or fifty men would not be likely to fire upon a single horseman whose identity they did not know, when they were waiting to receive a whole company of raiders.

I did not see or hear a thing to cause misgiving, and strode down the main street of Jasonville, which was well lighted, and went up the porch of the single tavern and entered the barroom. The bartender was off to the war, doing what he could for President Davis, and the heavy, waddling landlord was presiding, with two countrymen too decrepit to serve in the ranks sitting in front of the old-fashioned fireplace, smoking their corncob pipes. They looked up, but did not recognize me. The landlord, Uncle Jed, as he was known, scrutinized me sharply for a minute, and then grinned on one side of his face, as he had a queer habit of doing, came round from behind the bar and shook hands.

Uncle Jed was a genuine, old-fashioned publican, who felt that he had no right to hold radical views on politics or religion. He was equally friendly with everybody, but I always fancied that he had a special liking for me. So when we had talked together apart for some minutes, I asked him whether there were any strangers in town.

"No," he replied with another side grin; "about everybody except two or three of us have gone to war."

"Have you seen anything of Jim McGibbon?"

"He had a drink here one day last week, but I haven't seen or heard of him since."

"I understood he was in town to-night."

"If that's so I haven't seen him. It may be he's here. You know he's like you—he has lots of friends all over. I say, Jerry, if you haven't anything special on hand to-night, why don't you visit our lodge?"

"Is this regular meeting night? I hadn't thought of it."

"Yes; I'd like to go down, but can't leave the house these times."

"Are they working any degree?"

"I believe not; jes' the reg'lar communication."

Now, I felt quite certain that if Jim McGibbon was in Jasonville Uncle Jed would know of it, and if he knew of it, he would tell me. He was friendly to both, and if my enemy should drop in at the tumbledown tavern with an inquiry regarding me, he would learn the truth.

In my tempestuous life, I did not often get a chance to attend lodge, though I had been a member of the order ever since attaining my majority, two years before. A sudden impulse came over me to make amends so far as I could for my neglect.

"I think I'll drop in for a while. I can't stay long. Where does the lodge meet?"

"Just round the corner, down Lodge Alley. You'll see the lights on the second floor. Can't miss it."

When I presented myself and asked through the Tyler for admission, word was sent out that one of the brethren, having sat with me in my own lodge, vouched for me. Consequently, I was admitted without the examination through which I should have been compelled to pass had the case been different.

The moment the Tyler ushered me through the door, after I had been suitably clothed and told that the lodge was on the third degree, I glanced around, and saw that between twenty and thirty members were present. When the proper salutations had been made, the Master welcomed me in the usual form and invited me to a seat among the brethren.

Directly on my left I perceived a vacant space, with a large, burly fellow at the farther side of the vacancy. With a cursory glance, I dropped into this opening and then looked toward the East to hear what the Master had to say. It was at that moment I heard a queer, chuckling sound from the man who sat nearest me. I looked at him, wondering what it could mean. His face was so heavily bearded that I did not recognize him, but saw from the movement of the beard that he was grinning. Again, I heard the chortling, and he thrust his hand toward me.

"How are you, Jerry?"

You might have knocked me over with a feather. It was Jim McGibbon!

After our months of raiding and hunting for each other's life, we had met at last, but it was in a Masonic lodge. I had not dreamed that he belonged to the order, and, as he afterward told me, the thought never entered his head that I was a Free Mason.

"I guess the laugh is on you, *Brother* Chattin," added McGibbon, shaking with silent laughter, which, however, was so hearty that the Master gave a slight warning tap with his gavel.

"I'll admit it," I replied. "I'll be hanged if I hardly know whether I am awake or dreaming."

Despite our care, we attracted so much notice that McGibbon proposed we should withdraw from the lodge and talk things over. The Master gave permission, and we passed outside, down the stairs and halted on a corner of the street, where we were safe from cowans. Before speaking, McGibbon offered his hand again and we shook heartily.

"Now, Jerry," said he in his genial way, "I reckon things are on a little different footing from what they have been ever since—say, we played ball against each other. Are you with me, old boy?"

"I am, heart and soul," I replied with an enthusiasm that surprised myself. "I never thought you and I could be anything but sworn enemies, but now—"

"We are sworn brothers," he said, taking the words from my mouth. "I'm going to give you a proof of it. You have stationed your men a little way outside of town, with the intention of making a dash into the place and having a whack at my boys and me. You have come in alone to spy around, and when you found out how the land lies, you meant to go back and bring your chaps in."

"That is true, Jim; but how in thunder did you find it out?"

"One of my spies got on the track of *your* spy. How far out are your men?"

"A mile or so."

"Mine are only a half mile—hardly that, on the Turner road; they are lying in the wood waiting for your fellows to come within range."

"Then I must have ridden in front of them!"

"Beyond a doubt you did. More than likely, some of my boys recognized you. If they did, they kept it to themselves. You see," added McGibbon with another chuckle, "they're after more than *you,* captain. To make everything right, Jerry, I guess I had better ride a part of the way back with you."

McGibbon had left his horse not far from where mine was tethered. We mounted and rode out of town together, chatting over old baseball times and war matters as if, never a cloud had come between us. It seemed to me that after we had ridden some way Jim became more boisterous than ever. His laughter rang out in the still night air, and as he evidently intended, was identified by several of his sentinels, one of whom came forward from the darkness of the wood to learn the meaning of it all. "It's all right, Ben," he remarked offhand to the man, who saluted and withdrew into the gloom again.

We rode on until we were close to where my men were impatiently awaiting my return. I invited McGibbon to call on my company, but he replied:

"I wouldn't hesitate a minute, Jerry, with you, but it will be better not to do so yet awhile. Well, good-by, *Brother* Chattin."

"Good-by, *Brother* McGibbon. God bless you!"

So we parted. Neither of us uttered the slightest hint as to the future; it was not necessary. We kept up our raiding, but henceforward tried to avoid each other. We could not expect many of our men to understand the changed situation, and I know that Jim McGibbon purposely dodged a fight with me when nothing would have been easier than to bring the meeting about. As for myself, I steered out of his path several times when it had a queer look to my men. Finally, McGibbon made a shift of quarters, passing over into Arkansas, and thus relieved the situation of its peculiar tensity. We never met again during the war."

"Have you met *since* the war?" I asked.

To this natural question, Jerry Chattin made answer:

"If you ever visit the flourishing town of Jasonville, make a call at 234 Main Street, at the large grocery store of Chattin & McGibbon. More than likely you will find a big whiskered fellow smoking his corncob pipe at the rear and giving orders now and then, as if he is boss. Fact is he is half-boss, for Jim McGibbon and I have been equal partners for twenty years. He married my sister—the very one whose home he burned during those lurid days in Missouri—and their oldest boy bears my name. The parents of both Jim and me have been dead for several years, but it is pleasant to remember that Jim's father made his home with his son long after he had become a merchant. I can see that handsome, saintly face now as he looked from one to the other, and with his sweet smile and gentle voice said:

"'I was sure you two would some day become friends. I told you I meant to pray for it, and my prayer has been answered.'"

IX

A TYPICAL LODGE

IT would require many volumes to give even a condensed history of the hundreds of Masonic lodges in the United States and British America. The Grand Lodges represent a total membership of more than a million. They are in full affiliation with the English Grand Lodge, of which the Duke of Connaught is Grand Master, and the Grand Lodges of Ireland, Scotland, Cuba, Peru, South Australia, New South Wales, Victoria, and with the Masons of Germany and Austria. They recognize and affiliate with the Masons under the jurisdiction of the Supreme Council of France, but are not in affiliation with the Masons under the jurisdiction of the Grand Orient of that country. In Spain, Italy and other Roman Catholic countries, Freemasonry is under the ban of the Church, and the membership is meagre and scattered.

Inasmuch as we are dealing only with the Blue Lodges, an account of one will serve as an illustration of the history of all. A general similarity of the main features will be found, varied, of course, by local circumstances and surroundings. Those in the North felt little or no effects of the great Civil War or, as our brethren in the South prefer to call it, the War Between the States. But in their section, the times, to say the least, proved strenuous.

I select for my illustration Hiram Lodge, No. 40, of

Raleigh, N. C., and am indebted to Brother John Nichols for the facts, which follow:

This lodge was chartered in January 1801, and its connection with the prosperity and progress of the State for more than a century past has been marked. Many of the men, who became famous not only in the history of the State itself, but also in the councils of the nation, were made Masons in Hiram Lodge, No. 40. A history of the anti-Masonic excitement caused by the Morgan incident is given elsewhere. At the convention held in Washington, in 1842, Hon. Kenneth Rayner was the delegate who represented the Grand Lodge of North Carolina. He was a man of brilliant ability, an eloquent orator and a leading member of Congress for many years. He possessed considerable wealth, but all of it was swept away during the crimson years between 1861 and 1865.

In the political campaign of 1848, Kenneth Rayner was the competing candidate against Millard Fillmore for the Vice-Presidential nomination. They were warm personal friends and submitted their claims to a conference. Fillmore beat Rayner by a single vote. It will be seen that, had one of Fillmore's supporters changed to Rayner, the latter would have become President of the United States.

Thirty-three years later, Kenneth Rayner, old, poor and feeble, was Solicitor of the Treasury, having been appointed to the office by President Grant. When Garfield became Chief Executive, a persistent effort was made to have Rayner ousted. The hungry politicians were clamoring for his modest pay and would not cease their efforts. Garfield resolutely refused every appeal. Finally, a leading politician impatiently demanded:

"Why do you insist, Mr. President, in keeping in office a nondescript without any party, when there are so many good party men fully competent to take his place?"

The President's rebuke: "You are wasting your time coming to me"

A Typical Lodge

To this direct appeal, Garfield made the noble reply:

"Though he is an old man and out of favor with fortune, he was a host in his day. He is still an able and accomplished lawyer; he fills the office admirably and he sorely needs the salary. He may not have many friends, but he has at least one, and a mighty important friend, for it is I, and I am not going to turn him out. I will not remove from a little place in the Treasury, whose duties he fully meets, an old man who came within a single vote of filling the place I fill, and of being President of the United States. You are wasting your time in coming to me; I shall refuse to listen any further."

President Garfield was a Mason of high standing in Ohio. Perhaps that fact did not influence him in retaining Rayner. Perhaps it did.

The public school system of North Carolina was established about 1840. The success of the beneficent movement was largely due to the Masons of the State. The Grand Lodge in 1842 appointed a committee to inquire into the expediency of establishing a seminary of learning for the benefit of the poor children of the members of the fraternity and for such others as the means would permit. Some time later, Hiram Lodge, No. 40, pledged itself to contribute fifty dollars annually, in addition to the individual subscriptions for such purpose, the latter amounting to a considerable sum.

An interesting fact or two should be noted at this point. Down to 1844, nearly all the business of the lodge was transacted on the Entered Apprentice's degree. Members who were neglectful in their attendance were frequently fined, and it required a pretty good excuse on their part to escape the infliction.

Among the Grand officers who signed the charter of Hiram Lodge was Colonel William Polk, one of the bravest soldiers of the Revolutionary War. He was an intimate friend of General Lafayette, who, when he made a tour of this country in 1825, paid a visit to Raleigh. At the conclusion of Governor Hutchins's speech of welcome to the distinguished French patriot, Lafayette and Colonel Polk rushed into each other's arms and wept their gratitude that they, who had so often withstood the worst of battle together in their youthful prime, had been spared to meet again amid such peaceful, happy scenes. There was scarcely a dry eye among those who witnessed the touching scene.

Some of the oldest citizens of Raleigh hold pleasant memories of "Uncle Dick Ashton," who rarely missed a meeting for the thirty years preceding the middle of last century. He was Grand Tyler for twenty years, and one of the brightest of Masons, who was never restrained by modesty from assuming any station to which he was invited. He was popular with everybody, for his peculiarities were never repellent, and he had the kindest of hearts. He was quite advanced in life when the Royal Arch Chapter, which had been dormant for some time, was revived and the Chapter officers provided themselves with the gorgeous paraphernalia appropriate to their respective offices. Uncle Dick was the guard, or Tyler, for the Chapter, as well as for Hiram Lodge. When the officers appeared, "arrayed in all their glory," he was observed sitting at his station, with bowed head, disconsolate visage, and with no apparent interest in the brilliant assemblage around him. A Past Grand Master walked up to him and inquired the cause of his dejection. With a breaking voice and moist eyes, the old man replied in tremulous tones:

"I have served you all these many years; I have tried at all times to do my duty, and here you fellows are in your fine Sunday clothes and I have not been furnished with so much as a jacket."

A Typical Lodge

It was amusing and yet sad. The next day an order was given to a dressmaker of the town for a jacket and other garments for Uncle Dick. A member bought a broadbrimmed straw hat, then quite fashionable, and another picked up for him a rusty, old-fashioned, crooked sabre that had done service in the Revolution. At the next meeting of the Chapter, Uncle Dick appeared in full robes, and none was prouder or happier than he. The jacket, sword and hat are still the property of Raleigh Chapter, No. 10. They are carefully preserved among the relics, and have often been used in conferring the Past Master's degree.

The years between 1850 and 1860 were prosperous ones for North Carolina. Many public enterprises were begun and the resources of the State were rapidly developed. The fine building for the education of the Deaf and Dumb and Blind was completed and occupied; the Insane Asylum was established; the Methodists built a fine Female School; St. Mary's School was greatly improved; Goldsboro and Charlotte were joined by railway, making connection with other roads on the south and east; still other lines joined the Atlantic with the mountains on the west, and the public school system was thoroughly reorganized.

Masonry kept pace with these advancements. The membership of Hiram Lodge had doubled and its members were identified with the material and moral progress of their State. All was hopeful and promising when the dark clouds burst and the country was plunged into the greatest war of modern times. To quote Brother Nichols:

"States had taken up arms against sister States, citizens against citizens, Masons against Masons. The Southern soldier was captured and carried to Northern prisons. The Northern soldier in like manner was brought to Southern prisons. Many were sick or wounded or both. The signs of distress were seen in all these places of confinement, North and South. Masons all over the country, whether in the cold, desolate prisons of the North or the poorly supplied ones of the South, or in hospitals, or on bloody fields of battle, never failed to recognize the unerring signs of distress or the magic words of a brother's appeal.

"In the city of Raleigh there were several hospitals where the sick and wounded were brought for treatment. Among these there were, of course, a number of Masons. Some made themselves known as brethren, others were found to be such, while there may have been many who passed over the river who never gave the sign of distress nor received the fraternal grasp of a brother's hand. Of course, there were many deaths among them, and the Masons of Raleigh were called at frequent intervals to pay the last tribute of respect to a departed brother."

Raleigh was a recruiting station, besides containing a number of hospitals. In the latter part of 1863, a Mason's Relief Association was organized by Hiram Lodge. Its object was to look after the sick and wounded Masons and to provide, as far as possible, clothing, food and medicine for the needy. It was agreed that the Federal soldier who was a Mason should receive the same care and attention as the Confederate soldier, whenever it was possible to reach him. The existence of this association was known to Masons only. The good, which it did, will never be fully known in this world.

As bearing upon this interesting subject, the following is an extract from the *Key Stone,* a Masonic paper published in Raleigh during the war:

"*Masonic Dinner to Prisoners.*—On or about February 22, 1865, several hundred prisoners of war were stopped at Raleigh for a few days. A large number were quartered at Camp Holmes, and on the day designated the Masons who were prisoners, we are informed, were given a bountiful dinner by Masons of the guard who stood sentinel over them."

Brother Nichols relates the following personal experience:
"Among the sick and wounded Confederate soldiers in the hospital tents on the grounds of Peace Institute was a young lieutenant, who had been wounded in one of the battles of Virginia. At one time, he had been a member of my family. He was also a member of Hiram Lodge. Of course, I felt a special interest in him and frequently visited him.

"One day he said to me that among the Federal prisoners in a room in the building was a young soldier who was a Mason. I at once called to see him, and found that my information was correct. He had evidently been a handsome young man before sickness, although now much emaciated. From that time on, he did not suffer for any comforts that were at our command. In due course, there was an exchange of prisoners, and this young man and his fellow-soldiers were returned to their Northern homes. This was in 1864. In 1867, three years after, I was in the city of New York making some purchases in the line of my business. A tall, handsome young man was waiting on me in the establishment where I was trading. In the midst of our business, he stopped, looked at me and said:

"'Which State are you from?'
"I told him from North Carolina.
"'I have seen you before,' said he, 'but cannot remember where. I was in a hospital in Raleigh at one time during the war, and it may have been there.'
"I asked him if he remembered what hospital it was.
"'It was a large, unfinished brick building,' said he.
"'Perhaps it was there, as I sometimes visited that hospital,' I replied.

"Looking at me with his keen black eyes, he said, in a tone and manner that could not be misunderstood:

"'*Are you a Mason?*'

"I responded in the affirmative, and then he replied:

"'I thought it was you when I first saw you.'

"We then talked over some of the incidents of hospital experience, each becoming thoroughly satisfied of the other's identity. That night I went with him to his lodge, where, after introduction, I received a most enthusiastic welcome.

"I will not pursue the story further, but will simply remark that 'incidental expenses' during the balance of my stay in New York were not heavy."

Trying days were at hand for Hiram Lodge. General Sherman entered Raleigh on the morning of April 13, 1865, the advance under General Kilpatrick being the first to appear. The citizens hoped that the town would be spared, but were in dread lest an overt act by some rash person should draw down the wrath of the Federals, who were flushed with the decisive successes that had come to their arms. There was thankfulness, too, that the long, terrible war had come to an end.

Brother Nichols relates that after he had obtained protection for his family, as did many others, he set out with another Mason to secure, if possible, a guard of protection to Masonic Hall. The provost marshal to whom they applied was not a Mason and was not disposed to show the fraternity any consideration. While he was making curt inquiries as to the loyalty of the order, a young major came forward and asked the provost-marshal to assign to him the duty of protecting the interests of Masons of Raleigh. This was done, and not the slightest molestation of Masonic property occurred.

On Friday night, April 14, 1865, the saddest calamity

"You had better adjourn your lodge at once and send the brethren home."

that ever befell the American people occurred in the city of Washington. It was the assassination of Abraham Lincoln, the President of the United States. The following Monday evening, April 17, was the regular meeting of Hiram Lodge, No. 40. There were present at this meeting quite a number of Federal Officers—Masons, of course —and among them was the young major who interested himself in giving us a guard for the protection of our property.

The news of the assassination had reached Raleigh late in the afternoon of that day, and it caused a profound sensation among the Federal troops. About dark, there was a restlessness and spirit of insubordination manifested among the soldiers, and a riot was feared by the officers in command. In order to prevent such a calamity the guards at every street crossing were doubled, and messengers were sent up and down the streets to every place where the people might have assembled to warn them to disperse at once and repair to their homes. Hiram Lodge had just opened for business. Suddenly we heard the hasty footsteps of some one ascending the stairs to the hall, and the low clanking of the sword of an officer. There was a rapid knock at the door, and I was requested to go to the anteroom. There I met a Federal captain (a Mason, as I afterward learned, Captain W. C. Whitten, Ninth Maine Regiment), who hurriedly told me of the excitement among the soldiers in camp and suggested that the lodge be closed and that the members go to their homes at once. Orders were promptly obeyed.

There are a few Masons still living, perhaps, who remember that terrible night. I say terrible night because the impending danger of riot, murder and burning of the city was feared by every one who understood the condition of affairs. The wise and prudent management and strict discipline of the Federal Officers prevented what might have been a calamity of most serious consequences.

A few years ago in Washington City, I was in conversation with a member of Congress from the State of Iowa. Learning that I was from Raleigh, he told me that he came here with the Federal troops in 1865, and asked me many questions about the city and some of our citizens with whom he became acquainted, and related several incidents that occurred while here. Among them (which he told in a jocular manner) was that of two young brother Masons who came rather excitedly to the provost marshal's office seeking a guard for the Masonic Hall, and how quickly the lodge was closed on that eventful Monday night to which I have just referred. When I learned that he was the young officer that had befriended us I was as much surprised as he was to learn that I was one of the excited young Masons looking for a guard. It had been nearly thirty years before, and we had both grown older and much changed in personal appearance.

The gentleman thus referred to by Brother Nichols was Hon. Edwin H. Conger, then a member of Congress and afterward Minister to China. His confinement within the walls of Peking during the Boxer outrages, and the admirable tact and wisdom, which he displayed in that crisis that drew the attention of the civilized world, will be gratefully remembered by his countrymen. He died May 18, 1907.

In a private letter from Brother Nichols, he gives me several interesting facts, which deserve record in this place. His brother, P. Nichols, was a captain in the Sixty-seventh North Carolina troops. In the winter of 1863-64, the Federals occupied Newbern, from which point they frequently made cavalry raids into the interior.

Captain Nichols, serving in Virginia, obtained a furlough

to visit his family, who lived near Rocky Mount Station, in North Carolina. After spending a brief time at home, he set out on his return with a number of companions. Making their way to the station, they were waiting for their train, when a troop of Federal cavalry swooped down on them and made the little party prisoners. Before they could escape, they were hustled off and landed in prison at Newbern.

When Captain Nichols, who was of fine, soldierly appearance, made himself known as a Mason to several brother officers, he was paroled until the opportunity came for sending the prisoners to Johnson's Island. Before the time for the departure of the boat with the prisoners, the Masonic Federal Officers told Captain Nichols that he was going to a cold country, where he would need comfortable clothing, and that it would never do for him to take the voyage without considerably more than the poor fellow possessed. Therefore, they provided him with new shoes, a warm overcoat, two blankets and some money—all of which proved valuable indeed to him.

"I tell you," said the captain to his brother with a laugh, when he came home after the close of hostilities, "they treated me so well up North that I was half tempted to take the oath of allegiance and stay there; but when I thought of my wife and two little boys, who were likely to suffer because of such action, I determined to brave it out and remain true to my country."

Referring to Captain Nichols, his brother adds:

"He returned home a better Mason and a more patriotic American citizen. He spoke enthusiastically of his treatment at Newbern and was loud in his praises of the conduct of his Federal brethren."

It is a singular coincidence that on the same night that the Masonic lodges in Raleigh voted a subscription for the general fund for the help of the Masonic brethren who were prisoners at Camp Mangum, the Masonic lodge at Elmira, New York, voted a subscription to look after the Confederate prisoners who were Masons and were detained in the Federal prison at that place.

X

TRIED BY FIRE

IT may be doubted whether one person out of ten, if asked to name the time when the War for the Union was nearest to failure, would give the correct answer. Some would say it was directly after the disastrous Federal defeat at Bull Run, at the beginning of the struggle. But such persons forget that at that time both sides were in the flush of patriotic enthusiasm and the result of the Union defeat was to intensify the resolution of the North to press the war to a decisive triumph.

It may seem to others that the staggering blows administered by General Robert E. Lee to the Army of the Potomac during the repeated campaigns against Richmond marked the lowest ebb of the Union tide. Strange as it may sound, however, the darkest days for the National Government followed the most marked Union successes. Those days belong to 1864, a year following the fall of Vicksburg, and the repulse at Gettysburg of the finest army the Confederacy was ever able to put into the field.

And what was the explanation of this profound depression in the North and at Washington, when it looked for a time as if the war must stop with the Confederacy unconquered? Why had hope faded?

It was because of the awful price already paid, and the

certainty that still more would have to be paid before the end was reached. Tens of thousands of lives had been sacrificed and hundreds of millions of dollars spent, and the call was still for more men and vaster sums of money. Volunteering had given place to drafting, the government greenbacks had enormously depreciated, and the prices of the necessities of life were mounting skyward, with the certainty that each day, week, and month would make the situation more desperate.

"The Union is not worth what it is costing us."

This was the sentiment uttered by multitudes who until then were among the most ardent supporters of the War for the Union. They were losing heart; they felt the strain becoming too great to be borne. It is an impressive truth, which all thoughtful persons must concede, that if the stupendous struggle had not closed in 1865, with the Union restored, it would have stopped within a year with the Confederacy triumphant. I am sure that the most ardent ex-Confederate will join with us in thanking God that He averted such a calamity. No one can question the devotion to principle on the part of the South, any more than he can question the bravery of her soldiers, the ability of her leaders and the genius of Lee, her mighty commander.

None understood more clearly the real situation and the real danger than the immortal Lincoln. The furnace blast of trial had brought the real Union leaders to the front, and they, too, comprehended the prodigious task that confronted them. Despite the fact that the opening of the Mississippi had cut the Confederacy in twain, General Jo Johnston had seventy-five thousand men at Dalton, Ga., while Lee with a slightly smaller army, all of whom were fire-tried veterans, held the Rapidan River, as defiant and ready as ever to measure strength with the far more numerous Federal hosts, whom he had beaten back so many times from its advance upon the capital of the Confederacy.

At the opening of 1864, the National Government decided to make its campaigns against Lee and Johnston alone, all other military operations contributing to these two that were to decide the fate of the Union.

Hitherto the Confederates, operating upon inner lines, were able to reinforce any imperilled point. General Grant was given supreme command of the Union armies, and he determined to make an advance "all along the line," so that every Confederate force would be kept actively engaged and none could go to the help of the other. By such incessant hammering, the Confederacy sooner or later must crumble to pieces.

On May 1, 1864, the available military strength of the Union was more than three-quarters of a million men. It was intended to launch this colossal host against the attenuated armies of the Confederacy and to press them to the wall.

This is not the place for a history of the last advance against Richmond. Our aim is to clear the way for a Masonic incident or two connected with that memorable campaign. At the same time, it is interesting to recall those eventful days, in which the stake was so stupendous and the issue at times seemingly suspended by a single thread.

General Grant arranged with General Sherman that the general advance should begin on May 5. While the latter was boring his way through the core of the Confederacy, swinging loose from Atlanta and heading for the sea, Grant himself was to undertake the task of beating Lee and capturing the proud Confederate capital. It was Titanic work indeed, even with his overwhelming army and boundless resources.

In accordance with his far-reaching plans, Grant crossed the Rapidan on May 4. The fighting, which followed, was of the most terrific nature. For two days, the armies grappled in the gloomy depths of the Wilderness, and then the struggle was transferred to Spottsylvania Court House. Less furious fighting followed, and on the 28th of the same month what was left of the Army of the Potomac gathered near the Chickahominy, where McClellan had made his futile attempt two years before. There, on June 1 and 3, at Cold Harbor, the Confederate lines were assailed, and the Union army suffered the bloodiest repulse of the war. For twenty minutes, the losses in killed and wounded were at the rate of five hundred a minute! The Union casualties from the opening of the campaign were fully 40,000, that of the Confederates much less. The Union army was fought to a standstill, and when another order was given for an advance, it remained motionless.

One of the most gallant of the Confederate leaders, who was barely twenty-seven years of age, was General Robert F. Hoke. He commanded a division at Cold Harbor, and had received his commission as major general less than six weeks previous. Directly in front of his lines lay scores of Union dead and wounded. Loss of blood always causes a horrible thirst, and the cries of the sufferers were more than the Confederates could bear. Scores ran from the ranks, and, kneeling among the poor fellows, shared the water in their canteens with them.

They had been thus engaged only a few minutes when the Federals opened fire on them, not understanding the meaning of the charity. The bullets whistled so hotly about the good Samaritans that they had to hurry back. General Hoke was so indignant that he issued an order forbidding his men going out of his lines. In the lull that followed he lay down at the foot of a tree to rest, for the day was insufferably hot, and he, like his troops, was exhausted. While lying thus, two of his men approached, and saluting, said:

"General, a wounded Yankee is lying out in front and he wanted to know whether there are any Masons among us. We told him there were, whereupon he gave the sign of distress and begged us to go out and bring him into our lines. We replied that we had been fired upon while helping his companions, and because of that you had issued strict orders against our passing outside."

General Hoke roused up and looked keenly at the two men.

"Are you Masons?" he asked.

They told him they were.

"Do you know that it is almost certain death for you to try to give any help to that poor fellow?"

"We do; but he has made the Masonic appeal to us, and we only await your permission to try to bring him in."

"Then go, in God's name. I do not stand in the way of such courage as that."

As eagerly as if rushing to meet a returning brother, the brave men ran toward the Federal who lay helpless on the earth. They had hardly started when the enemy, still failing to understand the meaning of the act, opened fire on them. They did not falter or show hesitation. Every one expected to see one or both fall dead at every step, but they reached the sufferer, coolly held a can to his lips, and then raised his limp body between them. They walked deliberately back with their burden, and neither of them received as much as a scratch.

It is within bounds to say that instances similar in spirit to that which has just been related are to be numbered by the hundred. Scores who read these lines will recall them in their own experiences during the Civil War. I will add only a few, most of which came under my own personal knowledge.

Bishop E. S. Janes, of the Methodist Episcopal Church, was presiding at a conference in Texas just before the breaking out of the war. Feeling ran high, and open threats were made of breaking up the body, some of whose members were from the North. The bishop, one of the gentlest and most amiable of men, quietly went on with his duties, but warnings reached him that trouble was at hand. Sure enough, in the midst of one of their sessions Ben McCulloch, at the head of some of his famous rangers, appeared at the door. Standing just within the aisle, he called to the bishop:

"This can't go any farther. You must break up at once and leave. If you don't, the life of no man will be safe."

Bishop Janes from his place on the platform looked down the church at the stalwart figure and made a Masonic sign. It was done so quietly that no one not a Mason would have recognized it. McCulloch was astonished, for he was a Mason. Wondering how the venerable man of God had learned it—though it is not certain he was aware of the fact—he nodded his head.

"Have you any objections to our remaining in session until our regular hour of adjournment?" gently asked the bishop, amid the profound hush of the place.

"When is that?" asked the ranger in turn.

The bishop coolly drew out his watch and looked at it.

"A little more than an hour," he replied, as if holding a conversation with one of the brethren on the floor.

"All right; go ahead. I'll see you later."

I never heard how Ben straightened out matters with the clamorous crowd that had gathered outside, all eager to

Ben McCulloch, the Texan ranger, and Bishop Janes of the M. E. Church

BEN.—"If any one so much as says a mean word to you, I'll knock his———head off!"

BISHOP.—"Tut, tut, Brother Ben"

mob the clergymen within the building. Probably he did not have to straighten out or explain anything, for all knew the resolute character of that daring Texan, who met his death some time later in battle.

Bishop Janes despatched business with such vigor that a *sine die* adjournment took place somewhat earlier than promised. When the conference was breaking up, and the members were holding whispered and hurried consultations, the bishop observed the striking figure of McCulloch, who had again entered the building and seemed to be waiting to speak with him. The clergyman made his way down the aisle, and grasped the outstretched hand of the Texan, who said in a low tone:

"I saw your sign, bishop; it's all right; I'll guarantee a safe trip for you and every one outside the city. Don't you think it wise to adjourn without date?"

Looking benignantly through his golden spectacles, smiling and still holding the hand of the ranger, Bishop Janes said in his mild voice:

"Brother Ben, it *does* look a little that way. I have adjourned the conference *sine die,* and we shall wait until times are more favorable before we come together again. My good fellow, I want to thank you for your kindness."

"Oh, that's nothing. I'm sorry things are as they are, but it wouldn't do for these Northerners to stay any longer in town. I'll look after you personally, and if any one so much as says a mean word to you, I'll knock his——head off!"

"Tut, tut, Brother Ben. I have had a good many mean things said to me in the course of my life, but I forgive them all."

Ben McCulloch kept his word, and not a member of the conference was molested in the slightest degree when making his way out of "Dixie Land."

A friend of mine was taken prisoner with over a hundred others at one of the great battles in Virginia. After being conducted so far to the rear that there was no possibility of escape or rescue, the prisoners were drawn up in line, while their names were taken down and the necessary data gathered concerning them.

"While this was going on," said my friend, "a Confederate colonel stood a few paces back of the officer who was writing rapidly with a pencil on paper. The colonel was a fierce-looking fellow, and it seemed to me he showed a grim delight in contemplating our sorry plight. When each one responded to the questions that were sharply asked him, the colonel, with folded arms, looked fixedly into his face, but did not speak.

"At the moment my turn came a sudden whim prompted me to make a Masonic sign. I did it very furtively, and could not observe the slightest result. I concluded that neither the colonel nor any of his officers were Masons, and my little essay was thrown away. In fact, as far as I could see, it had attracted the attention only of Jim Baldwin, who stood next to me and recognized what I had done.

"'You are a fool to try that on here,' he said in an undertone; 'even if there are any Masons among these Rebs, they wouldn't pay any attention to you at a time like this.'

"I believed he was right, and thought no more of it. When our captors had pumped from us all the information they required, we were sent to our quarters and placed in charge of a guard. I don't think anybody ever felt bluer than I did. The prospect of a long, dismal imprisonment was before me, with the chances against my ever seeing home again. Some of my companions broke into defiant song and reckless jest, but I could make no such hollow pretence; I was utterly miserable and despairing.

"When the afternoon was drawing to a close, an orderly came past the guards and called out my name. Wondering what was up; I sprang to my feet and confronted him.

"'The colonel wishes to see you,' was all he said. He indicated that I was to follow him, and, still perplexed, I walked silently at his heels through the outskirts of the camp till he paused in front of a tent, drew the fly aside, saluted and announced his arrival with the prisoner in charge. The next moment I was ushered into the presence of the glum colonel, who was seated on a campstool, smoking a corncob pipe, and his expression seemed more terrible, if possible, than before.

"'What's your name?' he demanded, taking his pipe from his mouth.

"I gave it.

"'Are you a Mason?' he asked in the same crisp manner.

"I answered in the affirmative, and he then inquired:

"'Where do you hail from?'

"This was followed by the other questions with which all Masons are familiar, until I convinced him that I was what I claimed to be.

"The colonel abruptly ceased speaking. His sword lay on a stool beside his own. He crossed his legs and smoked furiously, with his eyes fixed on the opening in the tent through which I had entered. He seemed to be thinking intently, his face half obscured by the volume of smoke that continually rolled from his mouth. Suddenly he sprang up, and with the same brisk curtness, he had shown from the first, he said:

"'Come with me.'

"I followed, still wondering what it all could mean. He walked swiftly, and it was no easy task for me to keep pace with him. His course was such that we soon passed outside the camp, across an open field, whose fences, if there had ever been any, had served to feed the camp fires long before.

"By this time night was at hand—a night cloudy and without stars. My guide did not speak a word until we had gone fully a quarter of a mile. I remember thinking of a steam tug towing a vessel, as the puffs of tobacco smoke rolled over his shoulder into my face. Suddenly he stopped and faced about.

"'Yank,' said he, 'do you see that piece of woods?'

"He pointed ahead and a little to the right. In the slowly settling gloom, I could just distinguish the outlines of a forest, the farther limits of which were lost in the obscurity. I nodded my head and replied:

"'Yes; I can readily make it out.'

"'Well, run like the devil!'

"At the same moment he started at a rapid pace for his own camp. Not another word was said by him, nor did he look around to see whether I was acting upon his hint. In fact, it was unnecessary, for I should have been an idiot had I not 'caught on' and improved the opportunity that I may say was not wholly unexpected. Safely within the stretch of timber and some distance beyond, I had little trouble in making my way to our own lines."

At the battle of Bull Run, July 21, 1861, Edwin Cole, a private of the Seventy-first Regiment of New York Volunteers, was severely wounded and taken prisoner. After a short stay in Richmond, he was removed to the city of New Orleans, when Brother Fellows, then Grand Master of Masons in Louisiana, provided him and eight of his fellow-prisoners, who were craftsmen, with clothing, with medical attendance and with every needful comfort possible. In the excited state of public feeling at that time, the action of the

"Yank, do you see that piece of woods?"
"Yes, I can readily make it out."
"Well, then run like the devil!"

Grand Master was severely criticised, but the Grand Lodge of the State formally approved it, and in June 1862, the Grand Lodge of New York, by duly engrossed and certified resolutions, made its formal acknowledgments to the Grand Master of Louisiana for this most gracious proof of his Masonic charity.

Since this chapter consists mostly of detached incidents, I will close with the following: James Bellows McGregor, of Mount Sunapee, N. H., celebrated, September 6, 1907, his 106th birthday anniversary, and rounded out eighty years as a member of our order. At this writing (1907), he is in the enjoyment of the best of health, and the distinction of being the oldest Mason in the world.

XI

A LIVELY TIME

IF you should happen to be in the city of Providence, R. I., and should make your way to No. 19 College Street, and knock at the door of Room 18, you will be greeted by a cheery "Come in," and will find yourself face to face with a handsome, sturdy man, with a bright eye, gray beard and scantily covered head of hair. Although at this writing (1907) he is verging closely upon the proverbial three-score and ten, he is as vigorous, alert and wide awake as most men two-thirds of his age. If the great Civil War claimed its hundreds of thousands of valuable lives, it must not be forgotten that it saved many others. Those who in their early manhood passed safely through its perils, hardships and the rough out-door exposure became strong, rugged and tough. Multitudes of pale, dyspeptic youths who enlisted came out with physiques that laughed weakness and disease to scorn. They have lived the scores of years since in the enjoyment of high health, which otherwise could never have been theirs.

The gentleman to whom I allude is Judge George N. Bliss, but in his case, he was a splendid specimen of athletic manhood from the beginning. He is a native of Eagleville, Tiverton, R. I., where he was born, July 22, 1837. He was graduated from Union College, Schenectady, with the degree of A. B., in June 1860. Shortly after, he entered the Albany Law School, and on his graduation, in May 1861, was admitted to the Bar of the State of New York. In September of the same year, he enlisted as a private in Company B, First Rhode Island Cavalry. Young Bliss's ability caused him to be made quartermaster-sergeant soon after, quickly followed by his promotion to first lieutenant, which rank he held until mustered in as captain of Company C, in August 1862.

Having enlisted as a soldier, Captain Bliss set out to become a thorough one. He was a daring and skilful horseman, he had fenced with foils when a schoolboy, and became one of the finest swordsmen in the army. He was known as a man of undaunted bravery, always ready and eager to obey the orders of his superior officers, and never flinching in the face of any peril, no matter how great nor how hopeless the chance of victory might seem. Captain Bliss's modesty causes him to pass lightly over many of his exploits, which would have brought fame to any soldier. But his old comrades agree in pronouncing him a superb officer, whose example in the most trying circumstances was a model to others. He was a splendid type of the American volunteers, which have carried our flag to triumph on many a crimson battlefield. His qualities in this respect won the admiration of his enemies, with whom he crossed swords again and again in the hot conflict, which seemed at times and for so long to waver in the balance.

Captain Bliss's regiment was with Sheridan's army in the valley of the Shenandoah, and in September 1864, was on duty at General Torbert's headquarters, where Bliss was in command of the provost guard. After the victories of Sheridan at Winchester, on the 19th, and Fisher's Hill, on the 22d, General Torbert with his cavalry occupied Waynesborough,

Va. On September 28, they set out to destroy the railway bridge.

About the middle of the afternoon on the day named, Captain Bliss was directed by Major Farrington to ride into Waynesborough with orders to the provost guards to prevent soldiers from entering the houses, since the entire cavalry was about to pass through the town to water their horses in the Shenandoah. It was a crisp, cool day in early autumn, and the captain was in high spirits. A few weeks before he had been in the hospital, but the pure air, delicious spring water, good rations, and rough, out-door life had restored him to his usual perfect health. Life never looked more attractive to the young patriot.

The captain had in his charge about fifty prisoners, captured a day or so before. Just before entering the town, a sergeant was met with a large quantity of bread, which by orders of the captain had been baked in Waynesborough for the captives. Promising soon to return, Bliss rode into town to give his orders to the provost guards. Having done so, he was about to go back, when his attention was drawn to the efforts of a Vermont cavalry regiment to destroy the railway bridge. They had nearly completed the work before Captain Bliss heard firing in the distance across the river. Looking in that direction, he saw, about a mile away, the enemy driving in the Union pickets. The latter fell back to the reserves, which charged and drove the Confederates in turn.

Captain Bliss supposed the affair was only a skirmish, but when he saw the Union reserve hurled back, he knew it was an attack in force. He galloped back into the village, where Captain Willis C. Capron, of the First Rhode Island Cavalry, had command of about a dozen men as provost guard, and ordered him to form them in line across the main street,

A Lively Time

and allow none but wounded men to pass to the rear. This was done, and Bliss was on the point of returning to his squadron, when Captain Capron begged him to take command. Captain Bliss refused, but Capron insisted, and the faces of his men showed that their wishes were the same. They knew that in Bliss they would have the best of leaders. He read the expression of their countenances, and in his crisp, military fashion said:

"Very well; I'll take command; pass to the rear as junior captain."

At the same time, Captain Bliss drew his sabre and placed himself at the front. The firing on the opposite side of the river became hotter, but the Confederates steadily pushed the Federals back and the situation was fast becoming desperate. Seeing that something must be done quickly, Captain Bliss gathered about thirty men for a charge across the river, accompanied by cheering, the object being to make the enemy believe reinforcements were approaching. At the same time the main body of Union cavalry would be given time in which to rally for action.

The charge was made, and Bliss had nearly reached the front, when a major galloped up to him with orders from Colonel Lowell to take his command to the ford of the river and stop the stragglers. By his promptness, Captain Bliss checked fully a hundred and fifty panic-stricken men. With the aid of the lieutenants among them, they were gotten into line, when a Confederate battery began dropping shells among them. The whole body was terrified and dashed so tumultously across the river that they swept Captain Bliss's small force off their feet. He dashed after them, and succeeded in getting a few together, and began to throw up a barricade across the main street. There was not time to complete it, however, and the little body fell back until they reached the Third New Jersey Cavalry, drawn up in column of squadrons in the western suburbs of the town.

Looking again toward the enemy, Captain Bliss saw Colonel Charles Russell Lowell, who had been in command of the picket line, approaching with his horse on a walk. He was the last man to fall back before the advance of the Confederates. The bullets were whistling all about the brave officer, and little puffs of dust in the road showed where many struck. Captain Bliss hurried out to meet him.

"Colonel Lowell, I had only a few of the provost guards, but I did all I could with them to help you."

"There is no question of that; but, captain, we must check their advance with a sabre charge. Isn't that the best thing we can do?"

"I think it is."

A few minutes later, they came up to the Third New Jersey Cavalry. Colonel Lowell addressed the officer in command:

"Major, let your first squadron sling their carbines, draw their sabres and charge."

The order was given, but not a man moved. They were demoralized by having seen the troops driven back. Colonel Lowell shouted:

"Give a cheer, boys, and go at them!"

He and Captain Bliss set the example, and charged, cheering and waving their sabres. It was just the thing needed, and the squadron dashed hot after them. A little farther on Colonel Lowell drew to one side, so as to send other troops to the support of the squadron.

This left Captain Bliss to lead the charge. He was mounted on a large, powerful sorrel horse, which speedily carried him a hundred yards in advance of the others. Reaching the partially built barricade, he reined up and looked back. His men were coming on with a splendid squadron front, while in the other direction the enemy, in column of fours, were turning to retreat. It was the psychological moment for a charge, and Captain Bliss, waving his sabre high above his head, shouted at the top of his voice:

"Come on, boys! We've got them on the run!"

Touching spur to his horse, he went over the barricade at a single leap, and thrilled by the chance of routing the enemy, the captain put his steed on a dead run, and the next moment was among them swinging his sabre right and left, striking wherever he saw a chance of reaching a horseman. Almost in the same instant, he made the discovery that he was entirely alone. The men had not followed, and he was caught in the most terrifying peril of his life, for here was one man, attacking a squadron of cavalry single-handed.

When the fearful truth broke upon Captain Bliss, he had penetrated so far into the company that fully a dozen were behind him. They were retreating in a loose column of fours, and he had three files on his left hand and one on the right. He says that fifty men were shouting:

"Kill that damned Yankee!" and all set vigorously to work to do it.

Captain Bliss did not believe he had one chance in a million. He was certain to be cut down if he tried to retreat, and the farther he went, the worse would his situation become. In the dizzying whirl of the moment, he thought that if he could fight off death until he reached a side street he would spur his horse into that and try to make a circuit back to his lines. He set out to attempt the impossible.

It need not be said that all this time the captain was the busiest man that can be imagined. His saber flashed right and left, for he must needs, uses it with skill, might, and main to repulse the assaults upon him. He aimed one blow at Captain Morgan Strother, who dodged, and W. T. Haines ducked just in time to save his head. But Captain William A. Moss, Hugh Hamilton, color bearer of the Fourth Virginia Cavalry, Robert L. Baber and Thomas W. Garnett all caught it fairly and were wounded. (Later on, we shall explain how their names came to be known.)

While laying about him like a Trojan, Captain Bliss was on the alert for the side street to which he had pinned his hopes. He caught sight of one on his left, and dropping his head close to his horse's neck, he broke through three files, plunged into the opening and felt a thrill of hope; but at that instant a shot fired at him struck his steed and fatally wounded him. Feeling him going, the rider vigorously jerked the reins and struck his spurs deep into his flank. The noble animal strove bravely, but he was doomed and went down with a plunge, which flung the captain to the ground. Before he could leap to his feet two horsemen were upon him, and each struck a vicious, well-aimed blow. One used his carbine, and Bliss parried the stroke, which otherwise would have killed him. He had no chance to ward off the sabre, which inflicted an ugly cut on his forehead. Getting upon his feet, he called out:

"For God's sake do not kill a prisoner!"

"Then surrender!" commanded the horseman.

"I do surrender."

"Give me your sword and pistol."*

The captain handed the weapons to his captor, but had hardly done so when he received a blow in the back, which knocked him forward several paces. Turning his head to learn the cause, he saw that a soldier had ridden up with

---

*Referring to this incident, Captain Bliss in a letter to the writer says: "I suppose Shepherd, to whom I surrendered, did not dream how near death he was. If he had refused me mercy, I would have run him at once through the body, and we should have died together."

In dire extremity

"For God's sake do not kill a prisoner!"
"Then surrender!"
"I do surrender!"

his horse on a trot and stabbed him with his sabre. The captain grimly says that the reason the weapon did not pass entirely through his body was that the soldier, "in his ignorance of the proper use of the weapon, had failed to make the half turn of the wrist necessary to give the sabre smooth entrance between the ribs."

In the same moment, Captain Bliss observed another soldier taking aim at him with a revolver. In that crisis, when his life seemed scarcely worth a second's purchase, the prisoner made the grand hailing sign of distress of a Mason. Captain Henry C. Lee, the acting adjutant-general, instantly recognized it and dashed up on his horse, and peremptorily checked every demonstration against the wounded man. He ordered one of the soldiers to take him to the rear and see that his wounds were dressed. The order was obeyed, though on the way the prisoner was obliged to give up his gold watch, his money, and afterward to exchange his cavalry boots for a pair of canvas shoes.

Captain Bliss's wounds bled so much that he was too weak to mount a horse without help, but he was gotten into place behind one of the guards, and a ride of three miles brought him to a field hospital, where his wounds were dressed. Later in the evening he was put into an ambulance with Captain William A. Moss—at that time a lieutenant—who had received a bullet wound in addition to the sabre cut from Captain Bliss. Captain Moss, like Bliss, was a Mason, and did his utmost for the comfort of the prisoner. The sabre thrust caused the latter more trouble than the wound in his forehead. His lung had been injured, and he had to be plentifully dosed with morphine before he could sleep.

The next forenoon a mounted courier came to the hospital with orders to take Captain Bliss to the headquarters of

General Thomas T. Munford, commanding the Confederate force that had made the attack the previous day. The prisoner, however, was too weak to sit a horse, and the messenger went back without him. Late at night, the wounded were all landed by the cars in Charlottesville, and Bliss was placed in the officers' hospital. During the two weeks that he remained there, he was treated with every courtesy and kindness. The surgeon in charge, J. S. Davis, Professor in the University of Virginia, was specially attentive and did everything in his power for the comfort of the Union prisoner.*

A few days after the arrival at Charlottesville, a wounded Confederate called upon Captain Bliss.

"I am W. T. Haines," said he with a smile, "and was the first man you attacked in the ranks of the Fourth Virginia at Waynesborough."

"But you were not hurt," remarked Bliss.

"No; I was lucky enough to dodge that cut; if I hadn't, I shouldn't be here to shake you by the hand. No man ever tried harder to kill another than I tried to kill you, but your horse was too swift for me; as I followed, your sabre looked like a snake writhing in the air."

By the middle of October, Captain Bliss's wounds had healed and he was sent to Lynchburg, where he remained two days, going thence to Libby Prison, in Richmond. The long, hard journey from Charlottesville reopened his sabre wound, and he was placed in the hospital, which was located at the south end of Libby. He recovered so rapidly that in little more than a week he was transferred to the regular prison quarters, where he met an old college friend in Captain

---

*Captain Bliss informs me that he met seven Union officers whose lives were saved during the Civil War through their being Free Masons. And these were only a few among the hundreds and thousands on both sides.

Henry S. Burrage, of the Thirty-sixth Massachusetts Infantry, who had been unfairly taken prisoner several days before while exchanging newspapers on the picket line. The following day General Roger A. Pryor (now a retired Justice of the Supreme Court of New York) was captured in similar circumstances. Captain Burrage, on December 9, was summoned to the office of the prison and told that he had been selected as a hostage for a Confederate private, then under sentence within the Union lines. Captain Burrage reminded the commandant, Major N. P. Turner that General Pryor was already held as a hostage for him, and it was unfair to complicate his case by the new arrangement. Major Turner admitted the force of this contention and searched through the prison rolls for another Massachusetts officer, but finding none, decided that Captain Bliss, of Rhode Island, would fill the bill. Accordingly, he was notified of the unwelcome honor thrust upon him. Moreover, he was told that in addition, three other officers who were named were held as hostages for four privates that had been sentenced to be hanged by General Burnside for recruiting men for the Confederate army within the Union lines in East Tennessee. Captain Bliss was furnished with writing material and advised that if he wished to save his own neck he would better get busy and do what he could to preserve the lives of the condemned prisoners. With such an incentive, the captain promptly wrote to Senators Anthony and Sprague, who were equally prompt in interesting themselves in the matter. Few know by what a hair's breadth this delicate negotiation was carried through to success. Suffice it to say, that all came out right in the end, and one of the saddest of war's many tragedies was averted. On January 25, 1865, the hostages were released from their cells and sent back to the regular prison quarters. On the 5th of the following month, all, with the exception of

Lieutenant Murray, were sent down the James River on the flag-of-truce boat and re-entered the Union lines.

The experience of Captain Bliss in Libby Prison was interesting, but the story of the prisoners confined there during the progress of the war has been told too many times to be repeated in this place. The four months' confinement broke the health for the time of the rugged young man, and he was placed on light duty as president of a court-martial at Annapolis, Maryland. On May 15, he was mustered out of service and returned to the profession of law in his native State of Rhode Island.

The stirring events narrated were followed, as has been the case in many other similar instances, by a pleasant sequel. In June 1875, the Richmond Commandery of Knights Templars made a brief visit to Providence on their return from the celebration of the centennial anniversary of the battle of Bunker Hill. Captain Bliss had a cheery time with a number of the members, to whom he related his experience at Waynesborough. When they went home, they retold the story. Thus, the way was opened for not only an acquaintance with the ex-Confederates whom he encountered, but for the recovery of the sabre, which the captain had been compelled to surrender when, his horse was killed and he stood in imminent danger of death.

Under date of March 24, 1902, Robert L. Baber wrote from Rock Island, Va., to Captain Bliss, asking for his photograph in return for the three sabre wounds he had inflicted on his head in that lively scrimmage nearly forty years before. He got the photo and further correspondence followed. As proof of the truth of the account given of Captain Bliss's notable exploit, we quote from some of these letters. Mr. Baber, writing April 29, 1902, said:

"I was highly gratified to learn of the man who gave me such an awful drubbing, but proud to know that it did not

A Lively Time 161

seriously injure me: it only gave me six weeks' furlough. You say that three of the men whom you wounded after thirty years are still living, which is correct. Mr. Thomas W. Garnett is the man, if I mistake not, whose name you had not learned, who is living and whose post-office is Arcanum, Buckingham County, Va. Captain William A. Moss has been dead twelve or fourteen years, I suppose.

"I am nearly seventy-six years of age, have been a member of the Methodist Church nearly sixty years, was justice of the peace twenty-five years, a Mason nearly forty-two years and am a notary public now and have been for about twentyeight years."

Upon receipt of this letter, Captain Bliss wrote to Thomas W. Garnett, who answered on May 14, 1902:

"DEAR SIR: I am agreeably surprised to hear from you. I was at Waynesborough, Va., on September 28, 1864. I was wounded by the same man who wounded Captain William A. Moss and Robert L. Baber. (His name I have forgotten.)

"I received a sabre wound on my head. He or you gave me a right cut and passed on. I followed you to a left-hand street. I shot at you and your horse fell. Just then, Captain Moss called me to his assistance. I went and did not see you again until that night at the hospital. I was the first man you wounded in the fight.

"I got your sabre from Thad Sheppard and carried it the balance of the war, and buried it on my return home after the surrender.

"I never knew Hamilton. Captain Moss has been dead about twelve years. I know Barber. He lives about thirty miles from here. I am glad we are both still living. Write again."

Garnett set out to recover the sabre of Captain Bliss with the purpose of restoring it to him. Two months later, he wrote to the captain, telling him that after General Lee surrendered at Appomattox, General Munford called for men to go with him to join General Jo Johnston, then at Danville, Va. Garnett was one of the volunteers. When they reached Lynchburg, they saw it was useless to try to go farther and gave up. On the way back, Garnett was advised to get rid of his side arms, through danger of being mistaken for one of Mosby's scouts. Ten miles from Arcanum, he hid the sabre under the bottom rail of a fence, intending to return and get it after things had quieted down, but he never did so. The sabre was found by the owner of the place when removing the fence, and he notified Garnett that while he was willing to let him have it for nothing, it must be with the provision that it was for himself alone; but if he wished it for any other purpose, he would have to redeem it. Garnett wrote on July 27, 1902:

"I had to make the second trip to see Mr. B. F. Sheppard before I caught him. He said I was welcome to the sabre, but if sent to you, five dollars must be paid for it. I put the sabre under the fence April 11, 1865, and Sheppard found it in 1874. Nine years under the fence had left their marks. The leather on the hilt had rotted off and the scabbard was nearly eaten up by rust. Sheppard put a wooden hilt on in place of the leather, and used it to kill rats with, and cut off a part of the guard to make it handy. There is but one thing about it I can recognize, and that is the dent in the edge, which was in it when I got it." [This dent was made by the parrying of the carbine, as has been described.]

The old, battered, but precious sabre reached Captain Bliss a few days later, and it need not be said that no relic in the possession of the brave veteran is held in such proud and loving remembrance. It was on exhibition at the annual reunion of the First Rhode Island Cavalry, August 9, 1902. A noteworthy incident on that occasion was the presence of Color Bearer Hugh Hamilton, who received the warmest of welcomes from his former foes, but now his ardent friends.

A Lively Time 163

He was the guest of Judge Bliss. Hamilton is four years younger than the judge, erect as an Indian, tall, soldierly, courteous and strikingly handsome. The two had their photographs taken together, and under the picture, which is before me as I write, Judge Bliss has placed the following:

"Once foes, for many years past and for all the years to come, friends."

Captain A. D. Payne died at Warrenton, Va., in March 1893. In his account of the remarkable exploit of Captain Bliss, he wrote:

"The Fourth Virginia Regiment was at this point in the front, and Captain Morgan Strother, its commander, when he discovered the barricade, ordered some of his men to dismount to remove the obstruction. While this was being done, he suddenly gave the order for the dismounted men to mount, which was immediately obeyed, and just then, an incident occurred worthy of mention, as exhibiting a deed of individual heroism rarely witnessed. Just as the men of the Fourth Regiment were well in the saddle, after the order of their commanding officer, a single soldier, coming from the direction of the enemy, with sword in hand, dashed into the Black Horse Troop, which composed one of the squadrons of the Fourth Virginia Cavalry, and on that occasion was the color squadron, sabering the men right and left, wounding several, and among them Lieutenant William A. Moss and Corporal Hugh Hamilton, a gallant soldier and the color bearer. The boldness and suddenness of the attack paralyzed for a moment or two the Confederates, and in that interval, this bold assailant succeeded in forcing his way through the Confederate column, and might possibly have escaped, but a shot fired by a Confederate brought his horse down, and he fell with it. He was at once surrounded, and received a sabre cut in the face while in the act of parrying a blow from a carbine. Another Confederate gave him a sabre thrust in the back, and in all probability he would have been slain but for the timely interference of Captain Henry C. Lee, an aid of Colonel Munford, who, seeing the struggle, rode up and put an end to it. It is said that Captain Lee recognized in the prostrate man a brother Mason, through some sign or cry used by the Masonic order in times of distress or danger."

Brigadier-General T. T. Munford at this date is living at Lynchburg, Va. Writing on March 4, 1882, to Judge Bliss, he thus referred to the olden times:

"In fighting over our battles, as all good soldiers love to do with those who went hand in hand together, I have frequently had the incidents you recalled in your letter mentioned by those of us who witnessed it, and it affords me pleasure to say it was worthy of a better support than you received from the ranking officer ordering the charge or the men who should have followed. A little dare-deviltry in a cavalry officer sometimes acts like magic; a few dashing fellows well led have turned a victory from one side to a rout on the other, without any cause. Your courage will never be doubted by any Confederate who saw your manly bravery in the fight, and you may thank a kind Providence that you are now alive to tell your own story in your own way. You have spoken in a manly and generous way of what passed in our lines. When I saw you at night, sitting behind a Confederate cavalryman, with the blood streaming down your face, going to the rear a prisoner, I said to Dr. Randolph, brigade surgeon, that you were one of the 'widow's son party.' He being one of the elder brothers, replied, 'I'll see your mother's son well taken care of this night,' and as most of the staff-officers were of the clan, they did the best they could for a brother in trouble.

"I am not a Mason, but most of my staff was Masons, and I know they frequently did many things that seemed to give them extra pleasure for the unfortunate on the other side. I was sure the institution was full of good works, and although I was only a poor soldier who tried to do his duty, without being a Mason, I believed the organization was based upon Christian principles, and was always in sympathy with the work of the fraternity."

A Lively Time   165

In some respects, the most peculiar interest attaches to the narrative of Captain Henry C. Lee, for it will be remembered that he was the one who recognized the Masonic call of Captain Bliss when driven to the last extremity, and by instantly, responding saved him from certain death. Captain Lee at that time was in his twenty-third year, so that he could not have been a Mason for more than about a year and a half. He died in Richmond in June 1889. Some five years before his death he wrote to Judge Bliss:

"Just as Captain Moss got into town, owing to the Third not being up and the Second not well in position, I was sent forward by Colonel Munford, who was then commanding our brigade, to halt the squadron of the Fourth, and as I was galloping up one side (the right) of these squadrons (we were in columns of fours), I saw you galloping down on the other side. Knowing you would be looked after, particularly as you were alone, I kept on and halted the head of the troops, and then I saw your men going in the opposite direction. They were the ones you told me, when I first saw you after the war, you expected to lead in the charge against us and thought they were following you. My orders were also to bring our troops back that had been sent up on the road to the right, the First Regiment, for we were nearly into Sheridan's camp, and were fearful that your troops might sweep down this street and cut this party off. It was as I was returning, and had gotten to the corner, that I saw your horse fall and three or four of our men with you. As I passed you, you called out for relief as a Mason, and making a sign, which I recognized, I ordered our men to let you alone, take you to the rear and see that you were attended to, as you seemed to be wounded. I had to go on to bring our troops back, and, although you said something to me, I had no time to stop. One of our men was about to kill you when I got to you, and informed me that you had badly wounded Captain Moss, and had struck somebody else, and thought it wrong for me to interfere. When I came back of course you were gone, and the horse, too, I think, and I never saw you again until you came down to see me here in 1880. I heard that you and Captain Moss were carried back in the same ambulance, and Moss, having some 'apple-jack,' our national drink, you took a drink together."

In conclusion, it may be said that Captain Bliss received the Congressional medal for gallantry, September 28, 1864, and the records of the War for the Union tell of no exploit that was more deserving of the honor. Two of his sons served in the navy during our late war with Spain, and the veteran has long been a judge in the Seventh District Court of East Providence, R. I.

XII

THE MAN WHO SAVED PRESIDENT DIAZ

HOW the fate of the Mexican Republic once hung on the Masonic honor and fidelity of a Brooklyn man is the point of a remarkable political story that has been revived in every Brooklyn lodge by the recent visit to the Mexican capital of a member of Kings County Lodge, F. and A. M.

It is the story of a country made stable by the strength and ability of one man, and it contains every element of heroic manhood, unquestioned bravery, passionate politics and grim humor, running the gamut from the fate of a nation to that of a fistic encounter in which future President Diaz was sent sprawling across the deck of an American steamship by a purser who proved to be the greatest friend he ever had.

The facts given below are vouched for by leading Masons in Brooklyn and are in detail as corrected by the Rev. T. Morris Terry, of Kings County Lodge, a veteran member of the order and a Past Master. The member who is responsible for the revival of the story, because of recent honors extended to him both in New Orleans and in Mexico City, is another member of the same lodge, John Jerome Farley, an expert connected with the Goodyear (shoe) Machinery Company, now of 133½ North Front Street, Columbus, Ohio. Among those who have been prominent in an investigation of the story is Fred L. Jenkins, the head of the Veteran Masons, of 452A Hancock Street, Brooklyn.

Mr. Farley, however, though his recent visit to the Mexican lodges brought forth the story, was at the time of the series of events that are hereinafter told a babe in swaddling clothes in Brooklyn. Just who the real hero was is not yet disclosed, but on the statements made to the *Eagle* it seems certain that his identity is known to some.

In the early seventies President Diaz was not known as a patriot. Patriots in Spanish-American republics are successful revolutionists. Diaz was not successful in those days. Rather was he a fugitive beyond the confines of his own land, and few who saw him about the cafés and at the festivals of New Orleans paid much more attention to him than did men of later years to Cubans who talked filibustering in Philadelphia before the war with Spain.

At the time there was plying between New Orleans and Vera Cruz an American merchantman, taking to the warracked nation cotton, grains and foodstuffs and bringing back the tropical products and the mineral wealth of Mexico. The purser of that vessel was a young man from Brooklyn.

The purser did not know Diaz, nor did he know that there was a price of $50,000 on the head of any man in New Orleans, and the full knowledge of what such a munificent headpiece means did not come back to him till later years, when, tried by fire and found not wanting, he came to his reward by the hand of the man who, on that eventful night, he met as an exile in the Louisiana metropolis.

While walking along one of the city streets, thinking of the sailing in the morning, the purser was accosted by a friend who introduced a quiet-looking young man whom he asked the purser to make a passenger with him on the morrow. The stranger wore a magnificent Masonic emblem.

"He is a fugitive," said the friend, "and must return before it is too late."

The Man Who Saved President Diaz

"But I can't take him. My ship and my cargo might pay the forfeit," said the purser, shaking his head.

"But you *must* take him. He is your brother and his very life is at stake," was the stern answer.

The purser wavered and then consented, promising to protect to the utmost the stranger in his cabin from spies and Mexican officials who might be watching for the "rebel" leader.

On the morning when the ship was passing out of the muddy delta of the Mississippi, Diaz, who even for years afterward was unknown to the man who was befriending him, was seated at the purser's desk. He had been writing on a long, narrow strip of paper. Toying with it as the ink dried, he turned to the purser and slowly said:

"You have helped me, but I must tell you something. I am in your power. There is a price of $50,000 on my head. To earn that all you will have to do is to hold me until we get to Vera Cruz and deliver me to the military. Señor, you may do that if you like."

The young purser looked steadily at the man before him, started to say something and then stopped. Clearing his throat, he slowly and with a voice choked with emotion, answered:

"I don't befriend a man to betray him. I took you aboard. If I can, whatever the cost, I am going to put you on the beach in your own country."

Diaz's eyes filled with tears and all the fire of his ardent nature was in his embrace as he exclaimed fervently:

"Thank you."

The scene was dramatic, but no master of stagecraft ever completed another such with so strong a climax.

Handing the purser that long, narrow strip of paper on which he had been writing, the Mexican said:

"Here is a check equal to what they would pay you."

Again, the young purser looked at the man before him, almost angrily this time, then seizing the paper, he tore it to bits that were borne away by the lazy, sluggish gulf winds and lost in the wilderness of the blue waters. His answer was:

"I would not take you for money. I won't take money for saving you."

The next in a series of incidents in this game—where the life of a nation, rather than the life of a man was at stake—happened off Vera Cruz, where the American ship came to anchor.

"You must put me ashore," begged the future ruler.

"It's death, man," pleaded the purser. "I can't do it. If you are captured, I will be taken and so will the ship. And they will kill you."

"I must go! I will go! I will swim it!" young Diaz cried with that determination that afterward made him what he is to-day.

"It's madness, man. You will drown. The harbor is full of sharks. You will never reach the shore."

Diaz was obdurate, however, and that afternoon he divested himself of his heavier clothing, girded on a knife to defend himself against not only man-eating sharks, but also manhunting soldiers, and sprang overboard.

Taking to the water, he headed toward the beach, and the friend who had protected him so far watched him with his glasses as he rose and fell with the waves, now tossed on their crests, now hidden behind them as they broke in combers on the sand bars.

Suddenly Diaz turned back, and seemed swimming with redoubled effort to regain the ship. Through the breakers there plunged a boat and from it came the glint of sunlight as the red rays struck on the drawn swords of soldiers. The man had been seen and was pursued.

The race was an exciting one, but the swimmer had the start and was alongside as the purser shouted to the men in the fo'castle:

"Line the starboard rail! Lower a line," and made a place for that bit of the ridiculous that so persistently seems to enter into every affair of moment.

As Diaz was seized and drawn aboard the patriot soldiers were already coming up the gangway. The situation was critical, and a false move would have meant death to the young man.

Yankee wit, however, saved the day. Seizing the wet swimmer by his frowsy hair and giving him a heavy blow behind the ear, the purser threw him to the deck, and with an oath, pounced upon him and grabbed him by the throat.

"You drunken dog! You hound, I'll teach you to jump ship. I'll teach you to try to drown yourself," he cried.

Then, leaping to his feet, the purser gave orders to put the man into irons, and turning to the astonished soldiers, asked them what he could do for them.

In broken English, the leader explained that the country was in the throes of a civil war, and said that all ports were being watched for rebels, who had been driven from the country, but who might at any time return. Seeing a man in the surf, they thought that he had been caught, but were glad to know they were mistaken and that "Señor El Capitan had got his drunken sailor back." With many other apologies, they went away.

The next danger that menaced the young man was when two lighters came alongside to take off the cargo. These had aboard, beside their crews, emissaries of the government, and it was with a good deal of difficulty that the situation was met.

The work of loading was made as slow as possible, and it was long after dark when the scows were filled. Hiding the fugitive as best they could, the officers of the vessels invited the crew to share their hospitality while Diaz was rowed off into the darkness and put ashore farther down the coast. This effort was successful, but it interrupted for years the friendship that had sprung up between the humble purser and the great Mexican leader.

A few years ago, however, there came the climax, and it was brought about with all the dramatic effect of the modern melodrama. The sailor hero of this story chanced to go to Mexico, and among the places he visited was Mexico City. As he alighted from his train, he was suddenly arrested by military officers. Being innocent of any wrong, he grew indignant and begged to be informed of the cause of his detention.

"This is an outrage; send for the American consul," he cried. But the soldiers only the more pushed him along toward a carriage drawn by gayly caparisoned horses and gave the order to the driver to proceed. Bands played and the hoie poloi along the streets waved their sombreros and shouted. Being arrested with martial honors was something he did not understand.

His amazement grew as the procession drew up in soldierly ranks before the plaza and the American was politely assisted to alight and escorted into the central room of a palace, where there stood before him, dressed in a finely fitting frock coat, a thickset man of small stature in whose eyes he saw a look of friendly recognition.

An officer in uniform—still like the stage this story goes— then broke the clouds:

"El Presidente."

The friend of years ago, the exiled rebel, the brother in

trouble, was President Diaz, for years the head of the Mexican Republic. It all came back to him; even the head price was explained.

"But how did you know I was here?" asked the American.

"My friend, never since the day I left you have I failed to know where you were. I have followed you and watched you prosper. You saved me and you saved Mexico. I could do no less than wait for you to come back to her."

Recently the Masonic papers contained the announcement of the honors bestowed upon an American, but Brooklyn was not connected with the matter until the New Orleans and Mexico City lodges sent communications to the Rev. Mr. Terry about the visits of Brother Farley.

The Masonic announcement was, however, that the $50,000, which floated away on the warm waters of the Gulf Stream thirty years ago, was paid later as a present, and that an American Mason, the friend of President Diaz, was holding a responsible office under the Mexican Government.

XIII

ON THE SUMMIT OF THE ROCKY MOUNTAINS —FIRST MASONIC LODGE EVER HELD IN MONTANA

(Extract from Grand Historian's Address delivered before the Grand Lodge, F. & A.M. of Montana, by Nathaniel P. Langford, * in 1867.)

THIS brief contemplation of the leading features in our early history leads me to narrate somewhat in detail that portion of it which antedates the introduction of our order in organized form. I esteem myself fortunate in having been one of the early settlers of Montana—more fortunate in having, before I left the abodes of civilization, been raised to the sublime degree of Master Mason. When the company of which I was one entered what is now Montana—then Dakota—a single settlement, known by the name of Grasshopper (now Bannack), was the only abode of the white man in the southern part of the Territory. Our journey from Minnesota of fourteen hundred miles by a route never before travelled, and with the slow conveyance of ox trains, was of long duration and tedious. It was a clear September twilight when we camped on the western side of the range of the Rocky Mountains, where they are crossed by the Mullan road. The labors of the day over, three of our number, a brother named Charlton, another whose name I have forgotten

*Mr. Langford was Grand Master in 1869-1870.

On the Summit of the Rocky Mountains 177

gotten, and myself, the only three Master Masons in the company, impressed with the grandeur of the mountain scenery and the mild beauty of the evening, ascended the mountain to its summit, and there, in imitation of our ancient brethren, opened and closed an informal lodge of Master Masons. I had listened to the solemn ritual of Masonry an hundred times, but never when it impressed me as seriously as upon this occasion; such, also, was the experience of my companions. Our long journey and its undeviating round of daily employments had until this occasion had been wholly unalleviated by any circumstance calculated to soften or mellow the feelings subjected to such discipline. We felt it a relief to know each other in the light of Masonry. Never was the fraternal clasp more cordial than when, in the glory of that beautiful autumnal evening, we opened and closed the first lodge ever assembled in Montana.

Contemplating this early incident in the history of our order from our present standpoint, and including in the contemplation what Masonry has since done for the Territory, and the Territory for Masonry, it seems to have been invested with a kind of prophetic interest; especially as at that time it could hardly have been possible for the few Masons in the Territory to have known each other, except as mere adventurers. As a manifestation of the all-pervading affections of Masons for the lodge it is worthy of enduring record in our archives. It is one of those facts that will reach forward into our history and seize upon those undying elements, which shall transmit it to posterity. The fact will render the spot sacred—and once known among Masons it will never be forgotten —that the first lodge in the Territory was opened and closed upon the summit of the Rocky Mountains.

I might dilate upon the beauty of the evening upon which we met—the calm radiance of the moon and stars, the grandeur of the surrounding scenery. We exchanged fraternal greetings, spoke kind words one to another, and gave ourselves up to the enjoyment of that elevation of spirit which Masonry, under such circumstances, alone evokes; and when we left the summit of that glorious range of mountains, to descend to our camp, each felt that he had been made better and happier for this confidential interchange of Masonic sentiment.

Men when separated by distance from their homes and all that is dear to them upon earth, and uncertain as to the exposures and perils that lie before them, are apt to reflect upon those events in their past experience which afford the greatest promise or feeling of security and happiness. Every true Mason who has made the journey across the plains can attest to this. And as one of the striking evidences of the effect of this influence upon the Masons who came early to this Territory, I mention a little incident, which occurred while our train was working its weary way over the mountains lying between Deer Lodge and Bannack. I happened at that time to be the only Mason in a company consisting of ten or twelve men. We had stopped at noon for refreshment near the bank of what is now known as Silver Bow Creek, and were preparing to resume our journey when three or four horsemen descended from the mountains into the valley where we had halted. They were dressed in the coarse but picturesque costume of mountaineers, and presented to our inexperienced eyes the appearance of a troop of brigands. We regarded their movements with suspicion, and were ready at a moment's warning to engage them in hostile combat. All but one of them rode on without deigning to notice us. He stopped and engaged in conversation with those of our own men who were occupied in yoking our oxen.

I was at a little distance, and at the moment was engaged,

in adjusting the cincho of my saddle, when I heard him make the inquiry:

"Whose train is this?"

To which he received the reply, "Nobody's; we own the wagons among ourselves."

"Where are you from?"

"From Minnesota."

"How many men were there in your train?"

"About one hundred and thirty."

"Was there a man named H. A. Biff in your train?"

"No, sir; no such man."

"Did you ever hear of such a man?"

"I never did," replied one. "I know of no one of that name," said another.

Now, as fortune would have it, I had a short time before travelled the same road that had been travelled by the missing man (who, as I afterward learned, was a Mason), and I had been informed by those who at that time accompanied me that he had been killed by three ruffians. The particulars of his assassination are familiar to you all. This was the first murder of a brother of which we have any knowledge or record.

From the information thus received, I was enabled to answer his anxious inquiries; and as I rode along in company with him during the rest of the day, I was greatly pleased in finding in him an intelligent and warm-hearted brother Mason. It was his first meeting with a brother in the Territory, and we employed the time we were together in relating each to the other his Masonic experience, and bearing mutual testimony to the satisfaction we had derived from the order, and to its peculiar adaptability to our condition in this new country. A friendship was thus formed through the instrumentality of Masonry, which could not otherwise have found existence.

XIV

TRUE TO HIS OATH—A LEGEND OF THE NEW JERSEY COAST

REV. WILLIAM HOLLINSHED is a retired clergyman of the Presbyterian Church, and at this writing is proprietor of the Burnbrae House, a summer resort about two miles from the little town of Sparta, Sussex County, N.J. I spent the month of June 1906, at the Burnbrae, and formed a high regard for Mr. Hollinshed's ability and Christian character. He is one of the admirable few whose daily life is in accord with his profession, and whose retirement from active service, because of broken health, does not mean that he has ceased his labors in his Master's vineyard. He is as constant as ever in his works of charity, consolation and self-denial, and is known far and near as an earnest minister of the Gospel.

It was while sitting on the porch of the Burnbrae, as the moon shone over mountain and lake, long after all the other patrons were sunk in slumber, that Mr. Hollinshed gave me, among many interesting experiences, the following:

"I was resident pastor for four years in the Lackawanna Valley, where the Erie, Delaware and Hudson, and the Ontario and Western coal fields are located. My charge was the Forest City Presbyterian Church, six miles north of Carbondale and twenty-three miles from Scranton. The population of the section was about seven thousand. Twenty-five hundred men and boys were employed in the mines, of whom six hundred were English speaking, the others being Poles, Huns, Slavs, etc.

"My troubles came with the great coal strike, when a boycott was placed against the families of the pump runners, engineers and foremen, who were members of my church, and were trying to protect the property of their employers, make it possible for the country to have coal, and to save places for the workmen when the turmoil should end. These faithful employés were hounded, stoned and fired upon. They were refused meat, bread, milk and clothing, as were their wives and children. Out-of-town merchants were warned not to sell these necessaries to any of the suffering families or to their friends. The only way of satisfying their crying wants was through purchase by me in my own name of what was needed. I did this extensively, and distributed, so far as possible, the articles secretly, though it was inevitable that my action should soon become known. If there ever was a *persona non grata,* I was that individual.

"We must not censure the local dealers too severely, for had they disregarded the notice served upon them, they would not only have been boycotted, but that fearful agent, dynamite, would have been used against them. Although the woful situation did not last long, it was long enough for me to give some help to suffering womanhood and helpless children. I wrote to other ministers and a circular was distributed, asking for peace and an observance of the laws. It proved useless, however, for the men were in a desperate mood and a riot followed, which was prevented from becoming a bloody massacre through the arrival of the militia.

"The sight of my members, tried and true, insulted and pelted with chunks of rocks, filled me with righteous indignation.

In October, I wrote an article, 'A Voice from the Coal Fields,' which was published in the N. Y. *Sun*. Although I did not localize it, what I said was the simple truth. I was known at once as the author, and the mob became more inflamed than ever. The leaders of the strike replied with 1500 handbills of an inflammatory character, directed against me personally and meant to rouse the passionate hatred of the foreigners. Beyond question, it succeeded. I replied with dignity and courtesy, but it was like pouring oil upon the raging flames.

"One morning when I came out of my door I saw a book lying on the porch. Upon examination, I found that it had been shot half through by a revolver bullet, all the leaves had been cut by a razor and four grossly insulting messages were written within. I knew that action would follow these threats, but I was in the path of duty, and was resolved to go forward, content to do the will of the only One to whom I bow the knee.

"A few nights later, just as I had closed my prayermeeting, and was about to pass out of the door to go home, I was confronted by a woman, a member of my church, whose face and manner showed that she brought momentous news. Beckoning me to one side, she said in an excited undertone:

"'Mr. Hollinshed, you must not try to go home to-night.'

"'Why not?' I calmly asked, though my heart was beating faster than usual.

"'If you do, you will be killed; I am telling you the truth.'

"'I don't doubt that, my good woman, but explain; who is your authority?'

"'My husband; he overheard the plot; he was in the next room; he telephoned me ten minutes ago not to lose a second in warning you; I had just time to fling my shawl over my

"You must not try to go home to-night."
"Why not?"
"If you do you will be killed!"

head, and I ran all the way to this place; had I been a few minutes later nothing could have saved you.'

"When she told me this I understood it all. Her husband and I were members of the same Masonic lodge. He remembered his oath, and took his life in his hands when he sent notice by his wife of my intended assassination. His use of the telephone in the circumstances was dangerous, and his wife running through the wintry street was likely to draw attention to her, but neither of the couple hesitated at the risk. I do not mention the name of my loyal brother, for it is not necessary, and possibly might injure him, even at this late day.

"I thanked the woman and told her to assure her husband of my deep gratitude. It would have been imprudent for her and me to be seen together, and I waited until she passed from sight. Then I walked to the barracks and told what I had learned to the captain. He detailed two soldiers to escort me home, which was reached without molestation. The soldiers guarded my house for a week. While this precaution unquestionably saved my life, it did not protect me when on the street. On two occasions, the leaders shouted to their followers to 'kill the—preacher,' and they seemed eager to do it. On my way to the post-office one morning, I passed five hundred scowling men, with whom I saw I was certain to have trouble. In returning, a ferocious-looking fellow called me such a vile name that I turned to rebuke him. He was standing in the door of a saloon, and when I walked toward him, he laughed and dashed inside.

"By this time fifty rioters had closed around me. I faced them and told them to do their work. I preferred to die a martyr to American principles rather than live a craven and coward. The fact that it was broad daylight and we were on the main street made the mob hesitate, and I reached home unharmed.

"The nervous strain lasting through five months was too much for me. On the next Sabbath morning, I was stricken with paralysis while in the pulpit. What a proof it was of the reign of terror in that region, that not a physician could be found with enough courage to come to my assistance! I speedily recovered and remained two years longer at Forest City, myself and my church-members subject all the time to the boycott. The outside world can form no idea of those awful times. When the body of a workman was borne through the streets to the grave, it was between jeering crowds, who shouted, 'Good! Good!' clapped their hands, and called out the most shocking insults. It was almost impossible to get singers or pallbearers. Schoolteachers. Schoolteachers were discharged because they had brothers or fathers at work. Free Masons were too frightened to attend lodge meetings when their route led through any of the by streets, and it seemed at times as if no man was safe unless he meekly bowed to the will of the lawbreakers. I was no agitator, and never when in the pulpit defended corporations or attacked the Union. I did what I could to help the starving families of the strikers, collecting money, clothing and food, which I divided at the risk of my life impartially among those in need of them."

It was on another evening that Mr. Hollinshed related the following incident. While in pleasing contrast to his turbulent experience in the coal regions, it illustrates nonetheless touchingly the beautiful spirit of Free Masonry:

At the time referred to a prosperous cloth merchant of southern England lost his wife, to whom he was devotedly attached. Ruth, a daughter nine years old, in whom his love centred, could not dispel the gloom and depression of the father, whose decline in health became so marked that his physician told him that only a long sea voyage, with its change of scene and manner of living, would save his life. He reluctantly consented to sail to America. It was in midsummer, and his intention was to return home for the Christmas holidays. He embarked from Liverpool for New York, and almost immediately experienced an improvement in health and strength. When within a day's sail of land a dense fog settled over the vessel. A furious easterly gale set in. The captain lost his bearings, and hardly had the lead been cast when the ship was dashed upon the outer bar. This was before the establishment of that blessed institution of life saving along our ocean and lake coasts. The vessel was rapidly pounded to pieces. Nearly all were washed from the wreck and drowned. When all hope was lost, the father lashed his child to a plank. He had no thought that either would be saved, but he uttered a prayer that the body of his child might be found by some fisherman and given Christian burial. He pinned a little golden emblem, the square and compass, to her shawl, and had just time to kiss her good-by when the billows swept her from his sight.

A fearful crash followed, and the parent became unconscious. When his senses returned, he found himself in the cabin of a vessel bound for New Orleans. He had been rescued at break of day when the fog lifted. Upon his arrival at the Southern city, he read the accounts of a shipwreck in the newspapers, with the statement of the loss of all on board. He used every possible means to gain tidings of his lost daughter, but in vain, and when he finally sailed for England he was firmly persuaded that she had perished and would never be seen by him again in this world.

Five years later business called the parent once more to the United States. He had a vague hope that he might be able to learn something of lost Ruth, and that it should become his sad privilege to place her remains beside those of his revered wife. He knew the vicinity of the wreck, but when he visited it and made inquiries was not able to glean the slightest information. At the inn in New Jersey he learned that two of the guests were Free Masons, who had come thither as representatives to the Grand Lodge, which was about to convene in that town. Having made himself known as a member of the order, the father was invited to attend the session. He did so, and when the routine business was finished, he was invited by the Grand Master to make some remarks. He complied, speaking glowingly of the success and prosperity of Masonry in England, after which he told the purpose of his visit to that part of New Jersey. He gave a graphic account of his shipwreck, the loss of his only child, and said that the prayer of his life was that he might find her grave and be able to carry the remains to his home in England.

While relating his affecting story the Englishman did not notice that the Tyler was excused for a brief while, and that all the brethren showed a peculiar interest in his words. Recess was declared shortly after. A group gathered around the visitor and feelingly expressed their sympathy. He was in the midst of conversation, when suddenly a young woman was ushered into the lodge room, looked wildly round for a moment and then rushed to the astounded visitor, exclaiming:

"My father! My father!"

Before he could rally from his bewilderment, her arms were round his neck and she was sobbing with joy. Then he recognized her as indeed his lost Ruth, and every eye in the room was filled with tears at the touching meeting between child and parent, who had for years thought each other dead.

When something like quiet was restored, the Tyler in a trembling voice said to the visitor:

"This is the saddest and happiest night of my life, for I lose and you gain a daughter. I am a fisherman, and on that eventful day was repairing my nets, near the inlet, when the waves tossed a plank to shore near me. I saw the unconscious child and the square and compass pinned to her clothing. She was alive; and carrying her tenderly to my home, she speedily recovered under the care and loving attention of my wife. The Masonic emblem did not save her life, but it drew me more closely to her. I yield her to you with an overflowing heart; take her, but may I not claim that the happy daughter has gained a new mother and two fathers?"

"Indeed you may; you shall be her second parents as long as you live."

XV

A SOLDIER OF FORTUNE

CAPTAIN GEORGE B. BOYNTON was born in the city of New York in 1842, at 73 Fifth Avenue, just below Fourteenth Street. He received an excellent education, but when the war for the Union broke out, he was seized with patriotic fervor and enlisted in a cavalry regiment belonging to his native State. He fought bravely throughout the war. At the battle of Pittsburg Landing, his right cheek was cut open from ear to mouth by a sabre cut. He refused to stay in the hospital, but did valiant service with his regiment until the final surrender at Appomattox, when he was honorably discharged with the hundreds of thousands of other Union soldiers.

The taste of war, which young Boynton thus gained, has never left him. When he returned to his home he meant to do the same as most of his comrades did—settle down to a peaceful life for the rest of his days. However, a revolution began in Cuba in 1868, under Carlos Manuel de Cespedes, and Boynton threw all his enthusiasm and energies into it. He became famous as a blockade-runner. Despite the alertness of our Government, he got together many valuable cargoes of rifles, ammunition and supplies of war, and was equally successful in dodging the Spanish officials.

It will be remembered that though Cespedes captured the

town of Bayamo and the insurgents were victors in a goodly number of battles with the Spanish soldiers; the final result was not favorable to the Cubans. Captain Boynton saw that he would have to wait a long time for the money due him on account of the war supplies he had furnished. While he was meditating over the best course to follow, if indeed any course remained open to him, the Franco-Prussian War broke out. Believing there might be something for him in this new and more formidable conflict, he went to France to look into things. During that struggle, he brought several cargoes of war supplies into French ports, and on one occasion came very near losing his life. The Austrian Government was engaged in equipping its army with a new rifle. It had sold 3500 of the old rifles to a London firm, and they were to be delivered on the firm's order at the Vienna arsenal. Captain Boynton opened negotiations with the firm, bought the rifles and sent a ship to Trieste. When the rifles were safely stowed in the vessel, the Austrian authorities, not satisfied with the arrangement, ordered the ship to be detained. When the order was communicated to Captain Boynton, he replied that the officials might go hang, and directed the captain to steam away. Fire was opened upon the defiant vessel and she was struck several times. The wonder is that she was not sunk, but she succeeded in safely reaching the open sea. The daring captain deserved a better fate than to learn upon arriving in the harbor of Bordeaux, in March 1871, that the Prussians and French had signed a treaty of peace at Versailles only three days before. All the money paid for the guns and for chartering, the vessel was a dead loss, which fell upon Captain Boynton.

  Having the rifles on his hands, he decided that, instead of trying to deliver them in Cuba, he would dispose of them to Don Carlos, who was stirring up things in Spain, with the object of placing himself upon the throne. The Pretender eagerly seized the chance thus offered, and before entering Spain, in April, 1872, pledged himself to pay a generous sum for the rifles. The delivery was made, and Captain Boynton furnished several cargoes to the Carlists during the uprising, which continued to a greater or less extent for three years. No man could have been more intrepid than he. He bought several vessels in England and chartered others to be used in running the blockade. He had more than one narrow escape from the Spanish men-of-war, and came near being arrested and imprisoned in England. It will be admitted that the captain rendered the most valuable kind of aid to Don Carlos, and the pay, which he received for his services, was nothing. The infamous pretender, when he saw certain failure before him, not only refused to pay a dollar of his indebtedness to the American, but did his best to get rid of his creditor by having him assassinated. The captain was so indignant that he began figuring how he could suitably punish the swarthy miscreant.

Before a decision was reached, the war flames flashed up in the Balkans. He hastened thither, and fought with his usual bravery on the side of the Servians and Montenegrans against the Turks. Then the Russians mixed in, and Boynton, who had a large supply of war supplies on the vessel, which he had chartered to carry him to the scene of hostilities, sold most of them to the Russians, who were so pleased that they allowed him to witness as their guest the battle of Plevna. Then the captain returned to New York, but with eyes and ears open for new fields for his activities.

It looked for a time as if he would have to abandon the profession for which he had formed so strong a liking. The "Ten Years' War" in Cuba ended in 1878, and Spain for the time was triumphant. The Cubans unaided were unable to win their independence. They had to wait twenty years for Uncle Sam to expel Spain from the fertile island, and to present liberty to the natives, with the doubt very strong on our part whether the Cubans were worth even a portion of American blood that was shed in their behalf.

Captain Boynton was getting on in years, and after his tempestuous experiences, he had about made up his mind to settle down to the quiet business of life, when a quarrel broke out between Chile on the one hand and Peru and Bolivia on the other, because of the claims made by the latter two to the guano and nitrate beds on the borders of the three countries. The murmur of distant war was music in the captain's ears, and its beguilings were not to be resisted. He left New York by the first boat for Valparaiso, and most of his life since then has been spent in South America, where the chronic situation is that of revolution. For the quarter of a century following he was rarely absent from that seething continent, and in the history of the almost numberless wars his name will be found writ large.

Captain Boynton, however, engaged in a "side issue" which must not be forgotten. It will be remembered that Arabi Pasha headed an uprising in Egypt against foreign domination. He was defeated and made prisoner. Not deeming it prudent to let him remain in Egypt, where he was likely to make further trouble, England removed him to Ceylon. The deposed leader had many powerful friends in Alexandria, and with them, Captain Boynton made an agreement to take the exile back to that city. If he succeeded, he was to be paid $150,000. The veteran soldier of fortune made secret and skilful arrangements, for surely his experience ought to have qualified him for the dangerous part he had set out to play. In due time he arrived in Colombo, where the first news that greeted him was that the English had released Arabi Pasha. Thus, the grand scheme of the captain went up in smoke and he never received a penny for his part in the venture. Ill luck seemed to follow him persistently.

It would require a larger volume than this to tell all the stirring adventures of Captain Boynton in South America. He took a leading part in the uprising against Balmaceda, in Chile, in 1891, and eluded by a hair's breadth the clutches of President Baez in Santo Domingo, and President Hippolyte in Hayti. He made a flying visit to China, where, as was inevitable, he plunged into the fighting, which was then going on in different parts of the Flowery Kingdom. If he was unsuccessful in the way of making money, he was marvellously lucky in saving his head.

In the latter part of September 1893, the captain of the British warship *Sirius,* while lying in the harbor of Rio Janeiro, saw a tug flying the British flag, heading for the cruiser *Aquidaban,* the flagship of the fleet under Admiral Mello. This officer had joined his brother admiral, Da Gama, in heading a revolution against the government of President Peixoto of Brazil. The uprising was speedily put down.

The captain of the *Sirius* was at Rio to protect British citizens and property. That which he saw led him to believe the tug with its English flag meant to attack the rebel warship. He stopped it and demanded an explanation. Captain Boynton was in command and he was taken on board the *Sirius*. He declared that he was an American, whereupon he was turned over to Captain Picking, of the cruiser *Charleston,* who telegraphed to Washington for instructions as to what he should do with his prisoner. Boynton vigorously denied that he had intended to attack the *Aquidaban,* but was going out to Admiral Mello to try to sell him his cargo of war munitions. But Captain Boynton had a torpedo on board and had flown the British flag, which was a violation of the law of nations. Captain Picking was perplexed, and telegraphed to Secretary of the Navy Herbert for further instructions. It looked for a time as if international complications would follow as a result of Captain Boynton's activity. After some delay, the Washington authorities ordered him brought back to the United States, where it was hinted he might be tried on the charge of piracy. He was kept for four days at the Brooklyn navy yard, when the Federal authorities decided to let him go upon his promise that he would keep away from Brazil until the troubles there were over.

In reading of the experiences of this remarkable soldier of fortune—only a small portion of which have been referred to—one must wonder how it is he often came so near and yet escaped death by so narrow a margin. A partial explanation lies in the fact that Captain Boynton has been a Free Mason for a good many years. Many incidents in his remarkable career bearing upon this membership cannot be told, for reasons, which all brethren will understand. One occurrence, however, will be given and must suffice. At the time, he was especially active in Santo Domingo, he was caught "red handed"—that is, trying to deliver munitions of war to the revolutionists. He was tried by drumhead courtmartial and sentenced to be shot the next morning at sunrise. Captain Boynton made himself known as a Mason to one of the prominent officials, who was also a Mason. That night he succeeded in "escaping," rejoined his ship, and when the sun rose was sailing merrily away over the Spanish Main.

XVI

MY GHOST

AT a late "camp fire" of one of the army posts in New York, a number of veterans sat smoking and exchanging reminiscences. Two of them had worn the gray, and, therefore, were welcomed as warmly as they would have welcomed those who had worn the blue, had the situations been reversed. Brave men know how to respect and love one another.

It was Justice Wetmore of the Supreme Court who related the following remarkable experience:

"I have heard the remark made, more than once, that one of the pleasures of trying to kill all your fellow-beings possible in battle is the doubt whether you ever succeed in killing any one at all. You bang away as long as the thing lasts, but you don't know, even after firing a hundred rounds, whether you have harmed a hair on the head of a mortal. My reply to that remark is that I have positive knowledge that at Bull Run I dropped a Confederate and he never rose again."

The two comrades who had worn the gray were interested at once, as were the others, and asked for the particulars.

"You shall have them, for I'm in for it. I was the champion sprinter at Princeton, and if any one had any doubt of my ability in that line it would have been dissipated by my success at Bull Run. I was one of the first to strike a beeline for Washington. I knew the road well, and passed every one, streaking it for the national capital. The fugitives— and there were several of them—were so absorbed in getting away from the battlefield that they wouldn't clear the road in front of me, but I flanked all such and held the lead with little effort.

"I had no more than fairly gotten under way when I discovered that a long, lank fellow in gray was after me. That there might be no mistake as to his intentions, he shouted as he bore down upon me like a racehorse: 'You're my meat, Yank!' No mistake, he knew how to run, but he could not do more than hold his own without gaining on me.

"That July Sunday was a scorcher, and the Johnnies made it still hotter for us. Since my gun was only an encumbrance, I flung it away, and my coat, knapsack and other extras went after it. When my cap fell off, I didn't think I had time to pick it up, for all my efforts were needed in getting over the ground.

"I have always suspected that the Johnnies had arranged relays against me in that chase. When I had run about a mile, and looked over my shoulder, I was sure my pursuer was a head taller than the one who started after me. He looked much the same, except in height and the ferocity of expression: *that* had become more emphatic. At the end of the second mile, another hasty inspection of my enemy showed a similarity of looks except he was taller than the others. I fancied, too, that his cast of countenance had become more determined, so to speak.

"You will admit that it was hardly fair to ring in a relay like that when I was doing my best. At the end of the tenth mile, or thereabouts, the last relay began drawing up on me, and I had to put on an extra spurt that amazed all who witnessed it. Looking back, I saw the Confederate stagger; he took several wabbling steps, his knees knocked together, his tongue hung out and he groaned. Then he plunged forward on his face and never got up again. I had killed him by compelling him to put forth such terrific exertions that he couldn't stand it and collapsed. So you see there was never any earthly doubt that I had caused the death of one of our impetuous Southern brothers."

"What followed?" asked one of the smiling ex-Confederates.

"I have shown how I acquired full headway. I put on the brakes, but couldn't slow down enough to stop until several miles north of Washington. Then I managed to drop to a walk, and finally came to a full halt within the city limits of Baltimore."

When Comrade Wetmore had smoked a few minutes longer, he resumed in a grave voice:

"Perhaps I exaggerated a little in telling the last incident, but that which I have to relate now is strictly true and of an altogether different nature. When the war ended one million consumers were turned into as many producers, and you do not need to be reminded that they had to hustle during the first few years of peace. I secured an engagement with a large mercantile house in New York and was sent on the road to extend its trade. My intention all along was to secure enough funds to resume my study of law. My four years of outdoor life made me impatient of restraint, and I enjoyed getting out on the road and meeting so many old army friends, including those who had once been enemies. I had reenlisted after Bull Run, and went through the war until the final shaking of hands all round at Appomattox. I hadn't received a scratch, though I stayed with the Army of the Potomac and took part in all its battles. I became a captain, and when I laid off my uniform had stored up a reserve of strength and health which has stayed with me ever since.

"One autumn a lengthy trip was arranged for me by the house. I was to go to St. Louis, attend to some business matters there, and afterward visit the Southwest. San Antonio, Texas, was the farthest point, with a goodly number of towns at which to stop on the way, going and coming. I spent a week in St. Louis, and then set out over the Iron Mountain Railway, then broad gauge, for Texas. It had a miserable track in those days. The bed was poor, and we lost time steadily between the widely separated stations. I have often looked out of the last car at the rails and noted the ribbons of metal and the depressions, which made us bound and sway and jolt, as if we were going over a corduroy road. At your ablutions in the morning, you had to brace yourself, and were then liable to be pitched over on your head. I can well believe the remark of the testy old gentleman, who had tried in vain for a long time to read his newspaper. Finally, the car left the rails and began bumping over the ties. 'Thank heaven,' said he, 'I can now read with comfort.'

"From some cause, our train was held up for an hour at Jeffersonville. I was walking up and down the platform to stretch my legs when a bright, handsome young fellow glanced at the Masonic charm on my watch chain and with a smile remarked:

"'My friend, you carry good credentials.'

"I was attracted by his appearance and manner. Finding that he was a brother, we affiliated right off. He had been riding in the ordinary day coach, but I took him with me into the smoking compartment of my sleeper, and we spent several hours delightfully. He had been through the war, had been a cadet of General Sherman at the Louisiana Military Institute, had lost a brother at Vicksburg, and was twice captured, escaping both times with the help of some Masonic friends among the Unionists, for he had joined the order soon after the war began.

"During our chat and exchange of experiences we had one attentive but silent listener. Others came and went, but this man stayed throughout, smoking nervously and listening to every word. I took him for another ex-Confederate, but he was older than either Colonel Thomson, my new friend, or I. He was dressed in gray, wore a slouch hat, and had a full dark beard. His eyes were keen and penetrating and he had a way of looking intently at me that would have been disconcerting had I not been so much interested in my new friend. Even when Colonel Thomson was talking the attention of this man seemed to be centred in me. I was annoyed, but tried to ignore his discourtesy.

"At Marshall, Colonel Thomson and I were obliged to separate. I was going westward, while he was on his way to Shreveport. He urged me to accompany him, to cast business aside for a week or two; but I was forced to refuse. I am glad to say, however, that we have met several times since, and the acquaintance, begun so pleasantly, has been kept up ever since.

"When we were taking a parting drink of 'pine knot' at Marshall, and were about to shake hands, Colonel Thomson asked: 'Did you notice that man in the smoking compartment in the slouch hat and with the big whiskers?'

"'I did; he seemed to show a special interest in me.'

"'Well, I wish to warn you against him.'

"'Why?'

"'He is following you.'

"'What makes you think so?'

"'I noticed his manner in the car; a few minutes ago he slipped up to me on the platform and asked me if I knew your name? I replied that I did, but it was none of his business. I didn't like his manner. He then wanted to know if you had not been a Federal captain in the war, and if your name wasn't Wetmore. You see, he got it right somehow. I lost my temper and ordered him not to speak to me again. He muttered something, which I didn't catch and walked away. He is after you for some cause; he means you harm; be on your guard and don't let him get the drop on you. Good-by, my brother, till we meet again.'

"From that time forward the bearded stranger haunted me. He had probably learned my destination from our conversation, but at every station where I seized the chance for a little exercise he also paced up and down the platform. We continually met, and repeatedly I encountered those gray eyes, that seemed to pierce me through. He never spoke a word. Once, when I had become wrought up by his eternal shadowing, I confronted him, determined to demand an explanation, but he turned abruptly away.

"'All right,' I said to myself, 'I shall take care that you don't get the best of me.'

"Thus it went until I left the train at one of the Texan towns for a stay of several days. My shadow and I rode to the hotel together. After I had registered, he did the same without apparently noticing my signature, though I know he read it. He went to his room, which happened to be one floor below mine. When I had washed up it was about the middle of the afternoon, and I started out to make a few business calls. Glancing back, I saw him following a block to the rear. Coming out of the store first visited, after a stay of an hour or so, he was waiting on the other side of the street. He kept up his espionage, and that night at dinner sat behind me at another table.

"By that time he had gotten onto my nerves. I didn't

know how to shake him off, and I was too angered to attempt to address him again. For days, I had been trying to recall any incident of army life that would explain his persistent dogging of my footsteps. I couldn't for the life of me think of anything of that nature.

"That night I was so wrought up that I kept in my room, reading and smoking until a late hour, when I lay down to try to sleep. It must have been midnight before I shut my eyes. I first carefully locked and bolted my door, and laid my loaded revolver under my pillow. My belief was that the man had not yet found the opportunity he was seeking. If he entered my room and caught me unprepared, it would be easy to kill me and then slip away before his crime was discovered.

"I was in the midst of an uneasy, restless sleep when I was roused by a slight noise. I had turned down the gas, but instantly sat bolt upright, instinctively snatching my weapon from under the pillow.

"There he was, standing at the foot of my bed and scowling at me. He did not speak, but his appearance and manner said 'I've got you where I want you! Our account will now be settled!'

"With hardly a second's pause, I aimed straight at him and let fly. Then I leaped out of bed and made for him, pistol in hand. *But he wasn't there!* I turned up the gas and stared around. The room was empty, except as regarded myself. The lock and fastenings of the door had not been disturbed.

"I knew what it meant. My overwrought nerves had given away. I was deceived by a phantasm and was on the edge of total collapse. Fortunately, the report of my revolver was so muffled that it attracted no attention, but the remaining hours of night were horrible. I could not sleep,

"I aimed straight at him and let fly."

My Ghost

I shivered and trembled and finally broke down and wept like a child. I was in urgent need of medical attention and determined to secure it on the morrow.

"The landlord gave me the name of the foremost physician in the town, and I sought him out. He was Dr. Haskell, and not only was mayor of the town, but Master of the Masonic lodge. He had served as a surgeon in Lee's army, and was one of the finest gentlemen I ever met. He listened with keen interest to my story.

"'Of course you recognize that it is a case of nerves,' he said pleasantly, 'but I'm sure we can soon set you right. You tell me you have no recollection of this man until you saw him on your journey to Texas?'

"'I never so much as heard of him.'

"'Evidently a case of mistaken identity; he takes you for some one against whom he has a grievance; we must manage to set him right. Do you know his name?'

"'He registered as "J. J. Fanning," of Augusta, Ga.'

"The doctor started.

"'Describe him.'

"I did so.

"Dr. Haskell prescribed a sedative and to my astonishment said:

"'Go back to your hotel, sleep for a few hours (your medicine will enable you to do that), and at three o'clock you will receive a call; don't ask me anything, but do as directed.'

"Wondering and perplexed, I followed orders. The powders, which I took, induced refreshing slumber. When I awoke, I glanced at my watch and saw that it was three o'clock to the minute. I had scarcely noticed the fact when there was a knock. I sprang from my bed, turned the key and opened the door.

"And then you might have knocked me down with

a feather. J. J. Fanning, my ghost, stood before me. I was so dumfounded that I could only stammer, as I reflected that my revolver was in the pocket of my coat, which I had laid over a chair, 'What do you want?'

"'A few words with you, Brother Wetmore; may I come in?'

"And with the air of a Chesterfield he stepped across the threshold, hat in hand, and sat down in a chair.

"'Have no misgiving, Brother Wetmore,' he added in the same pleasant manner; 'I confess I did have evil intentions toward you; you once did me a great wrong, but I have learned that you are a brother Mason and *that* fact closes the feud.'

"'Who told you I am a Mason?' I asked, when able to command my words.

"'I visited the lodge in this town last night and made the acquaintance of Worshipful Master Haskell.'

"'But I never met him until to-day.'

"'He received a letter from your employers in New York a few days ago, in which they, or rather the head of your firm, who is an old friend of Worshipful Master Haskell, mentioned that you belonged to the order and would soon visit this place. I had a talk with the Master after the meeting and asked about you, not knowing that he had ever heard of you. He told me what I have just stated. I said no more, for I was thrown into a state of perplexity and was undecided as to what I should do. This noon the Master sent me a note insisting that I should call upon you at three o'clock this afternoon. He said it was my duty as a brother Mason, and here I am.'

"'I have known of your persistent dogging of me,' I said, having pulled myself together, 'and have been warned against you. I was prepared to shoot you on the first demonstration

My Ghost

on your part, and I am prepared to do so this minute. But, before going further, I demand that you tell me what wrong I ever did you, whom I never saw until a few days ago.'

"'Very well; you were formerly Captain Wetmore, of the Federal army?'

"'I was.'

"'On Sherman's march from Atlanta to Savannah he burned and destroyed right and left.'

"'That cannot be denied.'

"'He perpetrated many outrages, but as he truthfully declared that war is "hell," no special blame belongs to him. My paternal home lay in his path; it was burned to ashes; that, too, was only one instance of similar ones by both sides, and is not to be laid up against him. But a small brother of mine, only ten years old, while trying to save a pet pony from capture was shot to death by a Federal captain.'

"'It was an infamous crime!' I exclaimed; 'I hope he was punished as he deserved by his superiors.'

"'He was not; I took upon myself the duty; the name of the Federal captain, as I succeeded in learning after much trouble, was Captain Wetmore, of the — New York. You understand now why I have persistently followed you all the way from St. Louis, on the watch for a chance to shoot you?'

"I was thunderstruck. All was now clear to me.

"'Brother Fanning, you have my profoundest sympathy. I give you my Masonic word that I was never connected with General Sherman's command; I was with the Army of the Potomac from its organization to Appomattox; I never set foot in Georgia.'

"'Is that true?' demanded my visitor, starting from his chair.

"'As true as that I am talking with you this minute. My name is not a very common or a very uncommon one. What were the initials of the other Captain Wetmore?'

"'I never learned, nor did I try to learn. I simply found out his surname and that of the regiment to which he belonged. I need not tell you the unspeakable relief it is to know the truth, *Brother* Wetmore.'

"And we clasped hands."

XVII

REMINISCENCES

ONE cool summer afternoon Hiram Baker, David Payne, and Simeon Grogan came out of the hotel in Elizabethton, Eastern Tennessee, to the front porch. As each emerged from the barroom he drew the back of his horny hand across his mouth and sighed contentedly.

Every one of the trio was past three-score, lank, stoopshouldered, but tough, wiry and powerful of muscle and build. They wore slouch hats, hickory shirts, without coat or waistcoat, and the trousers of Baker were tucked in the tops of his boots. The other two had coarse, heavy unblackened shoes, and the hair of all was long and straggling. Hi Baker showed a grizzled moustache and long goatee. Dave Payne and Sim Grogan's beard covered their faces almost to the eyes and came down over their chests. In every instance, it was plentifully sprinkled with gray. Despite the rough, outdoor life led by the party, they certainly showed their years.

Hi Baker lived in East Tennessee all through the great Civil War, had scouted among the mountains and helped to burn the bridges of the East Tennessee and Virginia Railroad, an act, in the circumstances, contrary to the usages of war, and for which more than one Unionist underwent death by hanging or shooting. Dave Payne and Sim Grogan were ex-Confederates, who had helped hunt down the Unionists, and, incidentally, met with more than one narrow escape themselves while engaged in the work.

Hi Baker placed his back against one of the columns of the hotel, slung his left foot in front of the right ankle, and rested it on the toe of the boot. In this pose, he smoked his corncob pipe, thrust his hands in his trousers pockets, and bent his keen gray eyes, under his shaggy brows, upon the faces of his companions. Dave Payne crossed his legs, leaned back in his dilapidated armchair and smoked a twisted black cigar, whose odor was ranker than that of the corncob pipe. Sim Grogan rested his feet on top of the railing, and, taking out his jack-knife, slowly whittled a piece of pine. He was not smoking, because he had done little else but smoke since dinner, and didn't feel any special call to indulge for a coming half hour or so.

"Hi, do you know what this arternoon minds me of?" asked Grogan, contracting his left eyebrow and squinting at the neighbor who stood on his feet.

"I sholy don't," replied Hi, without removing his pipe.

"The burning of the railroad bridge at Zollicoffer."

"That was late in the fall, Sim, instid of summer."

"Ye're right, but the weather was powerful like summer fur a part of the time. I b'leve yo' had a hand in that, Hi?"

Baker removed his pipe and grinned.

"I reckon yo' ain't a thousand miles from the truth, Sim; I helped a right smart to send that bridge up in smoke, likewise several others in this part of the world."

"Who started the bus'ness, Hi?" asked Dave Payne; "I've heerd all sorts of stories, but warn't ever quite sartin; I reckon yo' oughter know something as to how it come about."

Hi smoked a minute in silence. Then he shifted his left foot to the floor and rested the other foot on its toe. Seeing

"Hi, do you know what this arternoon reminds me of?"
"I shorely don't."
"The burning of the railroad bridge at Zollicoffer."

that his pipe was burning so freely that it would run a while, he replied:

"It sholy oughter be knowed purty well; the chap who set the bus'ness on foot was Carter, the gospel sharp."

"You mean William B., of Elizabethton."

"The same; he was the brother of General Carter. The preacher was eighty odd years old when he died (July 1902). He took powerful good care to keep the names of us all a secret till long after the war, when no harm could come from telling who they were."

"The Yank government went back on you, Hi," remarked Dave Payne, with a chuckle.

"Yo're right; if we had knowed how we were going to be sarved, there wouldn't have been a bridge hurt. But we didn't lay it up agin the government, for you'uns kept it so busy in other parts that they couldn't send us the troops they promised."

"Reckon we *did* make things rather lively," remarked Grogan.

The statement of Baker, the Union scout, was true. The burning of the bridges of the East Tennessee and Virginia Railroad was the conception of the Rev. William B. Carter, of Elizabethton, Tenn., and was sanctioned by President Lincoln and the War Department, who promised to send a strong military force into the section, but were unable to do so.

I have not the space to give even a summary of the history of the burning of the railway bridges in East Tennessee. Some six or eight were destroyed, the work being carried out with the utmost secrecy, for those who took part knew the risk each man ran.

"Up to within twenty-four hours of the burning of the bridge at Zollicoffer (now Bluff City) only four men knew of it," said Hi. "They were Dan Stover, Sam Cunningham, Harrison, Hendrix, and his son, who was only a boy. Colonel Stover picked out thirty men, and I was one of 'em, though I wasn't much more than a kid at the time. All come from the neighborhood of Elizabethton, and we was swore into the military service at Reuben Miller's barn, at the head of Injin Creek. Colonel Stover explained the plan to us, adding that we was all to be paid for our work, and General Thomas, who was believed to be near the borders of East Tennessee, would advance to our protection, finish the destruction of the bridges and take care of all of us against you Johnnies. Wal, as I remarked, he didn't do it.

"Doc Cameron furnished the turpentine, and we had about a cord of fat pine knots with us. We crossed the Watauga at Drake's Ford, a mile east of Elizabethton, went through Turkey Town and down Injin Creek, where some more men j'ined us. When we got within a half mile of Zollicoffer, we halted and dismounted near a stretch of woods. The horses was hidden and guarded by Elijah Simerley, Pleasant Williams, and Ben Treadway. Colonel Stover told the men what was to be done, and said he wished no one to go with him who was afraid of the risk he would have to run. Several fell out of line. Colonel Stover and Gilson Collins had masks over their faces, but no others of us were disguised in any way.

"We went forward like so many Injin scouts. Reaching the south end of the bridge, we didn't see any guards at first. There some of the men were faced up the river and others down the river. I was one of the six or eight who hurried through the bridge almost to the north end. Two guards were under the bridge. Finding themselves caught, they surrendered and begged not to be shot. Several of our men wished to kill them, but the officers wouldn't allow it.

"Wal, the bus'ness didn't take us long. We made a big pile of knots, poured the turpentine over 'em, touched 'em off and then hurried back to where we had left our horses. We took one of the guards with us."

"He was that onery cuss, —— ——," interrupted Dave Payne.

"He was that identical dog. There wasn't any doubt that he had recognized several of us. We hadn't rode far when we stopped to decide what to do with him. One of our party was Jonas Keen. —— had once worked for him, and the two spoke to each other as old acquaintances. Nearly all the party urged that——should be shot. They said he would be sure to betray us if released, and their lives would pay for it. Two things saved him. Keen himself interceded for him, and the cur dropped on his knees, swore that nothing in the world could induce him to give us away, and begged and whined and made so many promises that we let him go."

"And how did he sarve yo'?" asked Grogan with another grin.

"As soon as he got out of our reach, he nearly broke his neck hurrying back to your lines, where he told the name of every one that he knew, and, to make good measure, added the names of several chaps who warn't with us."

At this point in his story, Hi Baker found his pipe had been neglected so long that the fire was out. He drew a big match, with its trailing line of sulphur smoke, along the sides of his linsey-woolseys, punched down the tobacco with his forefinger, and smoked so vigorously that the tiny flame quickly caught. Observing the interested expression on the faces of his friends, he continued:

"—— made oath of his story to the Confederate authorities. The first man arrested was young Hendrix. Although he, afterward the captain, as you know, was one of the most active in burning the Zollicoffer Bridge, he offered a good alibi, and was released under promise to stay within the Confederate lines and to report twice a day. He broke his promise, got away, and warned Keen and others of their danger in time for them to escape."

"What yo' say about —— is right," remarked Payne. "I was nigh enough to hear him swear to the names of the chaps that burned that bridge. Yours was among 'em."

"I knowed it," said Baker, "and you started out to fetch me in."

"Correct agin, except so fur as fetching in; them was the *official* orders, but it was understood that we needn't be very partic'lar about fetching yo' in, so we got yo'."

"Of course, that was the rule on each side; it was so easy to draw bead onto a chap and give him the witch's parole that it was done oftener than most folks think. If I ain't mistook, Dave," said Hi with a grin, "yo' come nigh gettin' me too."

"As sure as a gun. Up in the Gap, just at dusk, I seen yo' a-settin' on a log, and not thinking nothing. How was it, Hi, that jest as I war bringing my old Betsey to a level you dropped on tother side of the old tree, where I couldn't get a show at yo'?"

Baker laughed.

"I fell off; I was clean worn out; I'd been on the tramp for the most of two days and nights, and when I nodded a leetle too much, I dived off the log, kerflummix to the ground. That made me wide-awake. I sorter felt it was a warning, and I peeped over the tree to larn whether anything wrong was going on. I catched a glimpse of yo' standing up and looking round, as if yo' didn't understand what it all meant. Then I drawed bead on yo' and let fly, but I was in too much of a hurry, and too tired to make good aim."

"Yo' come as near as I cared to have yo' come; see that?"

Payne turned his head sideways and pulled at the lobe of his ear. A piece the size of a dime had been nipped off many a long year before.

"Couldn't have come much nigher without h'isting me over the big Divide."

"Does look a leetle that way," commented Baker, resuming his smoke.

Grogan slowly let down his feet from the railing, stopped whittling, resting his elbows on the arms of the chair, so that his shoulders were hunched up, twisted down his left eyebrow, as he was in the habit of doing, and drawled:

"Things were powerful mixed in these parts during them times. Yo' shorely didn't know who yo' could trust. Me and Jim Dady took each other for home-bred Yanks, and didn't find out our mistake till we had exchanged three shots and I catched him in the leg."

"I reckon, Sim, there warn't no mistake when you and Dick Swinton and Bob Orrix set out to scoop me in, eh, Sim?" asked Baker.

"There was the biggest kind of a mistake, Hi; we three was laying 'long the road not a half mile from Carter's Station, waiting for yo', for we knowed it was about time for yo' to visit yo'r home to see the old folks. It was so near dark that we couldn't see very plain, but we was all shore it was yo'rself when yo' rid round the corner jest beyant that patch o' woods. I riz up and sung out for yo' to throw up yo'r hands, but yo' turned and dashed off, as hard as yo'r critter could go. The other two fired; I'd done the same, but yo' pitched out of the saddle afore I could draw bead.

We run forrid from where we was laying in ambush, and when we got to the side of the road, with yo'r horse running like mad, we seed it warn't yo', but Len Demarest, one of our own friends."

"I've herd of that little mistake, Sim; it was lucky for me that Len Demarest went up the road the day ahead of me, for I was close behind."

"Yes; lucky for yo', but not very lucky for Len," said Grogan grimly; "Len was one of the hottest secesh in Tennessee, and expected to be app'inted a captain that same week. We was mighty cut up over it. After talking it over, it was agreed that Dick and Bob would tote the body home, while I went ahead and made it right with his ole woman. I couldn't think of what was best to say, but when I seen his wife washing in her front yard I talked with her a few minutes, keeping putting off the unpleasant duty, till I catched sight of Dick and Bob coming up the road with the body. Then I braced and told her I had to apologize for a little mistake we boys had made, but it looked to me as if she had the laugh onto us. We'd shot her husband Len by mistake for Hi Baker. She remarked that we oughter be ashamed of ourselves for being such fools, and then resumed her washing. Howsumever," added Grogan, with a lugubrious look and a deep sigh, "the widder got her revenge onto me."

"How?"

"She married me. Boys, let's have a drink!"

XVIII

"FOR GOD'S SAKE, 'LIGE, FLEE TO THE MOUNTAINS!"

[The following facts were given to me by my friend and neighbor, Mrs. Jennie Badgley, wife of Mr. Alfred S. Badgley, the well-known lawyer of Montclair; N. J. Mrs. Badgley is the oldest daughter of the late Elijah Simerley, of East Tennessee, who played so important a part in the incidents that follow.]

EAST TENNESSEE is one of the most picturesque and romantic regions in the world. It well deserves the name of the Switzerland of America. The Appalachian range separates the State from North Carolina and is there known as the Unaka or Smoky Mountains. Mount Guyot, the loftiest peak, rises 6,636 feet above the sea level. West of these mountains and including the Cumberland Plateau stretches the beautiful and salubrious valley of East Tennessee. Numerous rivers and streams of sparkling water frolic through the mountainous region and give the section a wondrous attractiveness that makes it the dream of the artist and tourist.

The East Tennessee and Western North Carolina Railroad, popularly known as the Cranberry line, winds through one of the most delightful regions in our country. The first ten miles, connecting Johnson City and Elizabethton, crosses the fertile portion of the lower Wautaga. It was in that section that Andrew Johnson, though a native of North Carolina began the remarkable political career, which finally carried him into the White House. There was born and reared the great jurist Thomas A. R. Nelson. In the same valley, Colonels Shelby and Sevier gathered the unerring riflemen with whom they won the victory at King's Mountain, in the autumn of 1780. William Gannaway Brownlow, the "fighting parson," preached and ran a forge and a casting furnace on the Doe River. Near at hand Andrew Jackson held the first Supreme Court ever convened in Tennessee. Almost within stone's throw of the spot, the Taylor brothers, Alf and Bob, lived and were rival candidates for governor in 1886. It was Bob who said he meant to retire, when through with politics, to East Tennessee, there to lie on his back in the fragrant grass, look up into the blue sky and tickle the toes of the angels.

To paraphrase a declaration of Parson Brownlow, the nearest point to hell ever attained by our beloved country was reached in this same East Tennessee during the crimson years of the Civil War. This was especially true in the early months of the mighty struggle.

Those who lived in the distinctively Northern or Southern States can form only a faint idea of the terrifying conditions in the Border States, where the sentiment was divided. War is the curse of mankind, and always brings out the most vicious side of human nature. The Hon. Champ Clark, referring to Missouri, said:

"The war was waged with unspeakable bitterness, sometimes with inhuman cruelty. It was fought by men in single combat, in squads, in companies, in regiments, in the fields, in fortified towns and in ambush, under the Stars and Stripes, under the Stars and Bars, and under the black flag. The arch fiend himself seems to have been on the field in person, inspiring, directing, and commanding."

This description fitted East Tennessee exactly. There the majority of the people were Union, as was the case in western North Carolina, which touched Tennessee. The mountaineers of those sections raised no cotton and felt no sympathy with slavery. As one moved westward, however, the secession sentiment deepened, and finally became dominant in middle and western Tennessee.

An overwhelming majority in middle and western Tennessee voted for secession, but in East Tennessee, there was a surplus of twenty thousand votes cast against it. On June 24th, Governor Harris issued a proclamation, dissolving the relations of Tennessee with the Federal Government. To show the mixed state of affairs, in August following Thomas A. R. Nelson, Horace Maynard, and G. W. Bridges were elected as representatives to the United States Congress, while others were chosen at the same time as members of the Confederate Congress. Judge Nelson was captured on his way to Washington and sent as a political prisoner to Richmond, but was soon after paroled and released.

Amid this wrangling, turmoil and strife, East Tennessee stood like a rock for the Union. She would not have dared to do so but for the pledge of support made by the Federal Government. It was this promise that, as has been already said, gave the bridge burners the heart to do their dangerous work. The stress of war postponed the fulfilment of the Government's promise for many weary months. Then it was that East Tennessee entered upon that existence which justified the words of Parson Brownlow.

Carter and Johnson form the extreme eastern counties of Tennessee. Colonel N. G. Taylor after the close of the war began an investigation into the tragedies that had occurred in that section. He did not complete his work, but advanced far enough to learn that there had been more than two hundred of them in the two counties named. It is not well to dwell upon or to recall these dreadful occurrences. Let us seek rather to show the better side of human nature, as it was shown many a time and oft during those days of sorrow, suffering and strife.

The most famous scout and guide developed by those years was Captain Daniel Ellis, a native of Carter County. He was not quite thirty-four years old when the war broke out. He had served against Mexico, and was a wonderful hunter and woodsman. The signs and mute language of the woods were an open book to him, and no man had a more intimate knowledge of that wild section. In the course of the war, he piloted more than four thousand persons from East Tennessee, Southwest Virginia and western North Carolina into the Union lines. The most vivid imagination can picture no more thrilling adventures than those of this remarkable man. He entered the military service toward the close of the war, and displayed the same nerve, coolness and daring that he had shown from the first and in all circumstances. Captain Daniel Ellis died at his home, Hampton, Tennessee, January 6, 1908. One of his sons is a practicing physician there and another is a member of the County Court.

Few people suspect the beneficent part played by Free Masonry during those horrifying days in East Tennessee (and in all parts of the country as well). Among the numerous instances, I recall that of Albert D. Richardson, correspondent of the *New York Tribune.* In the month of May 1863, he and several others, while trying to float past the Vicksburg batteries, were captured by the Confederates. After spending twenty months in different prisons, he succeeded in escaping from that at Salisbury, N. C., and started

"For God's Sake, 'Lige, Flee to the Mountains!"   223

on his long and dangerous tramp in the depth of winter to the Union lines. With the help of Dan Ellis and others, he managed to reach East Tennessee. He never could have gotten any farther but for the aid of brother Masons, some of whom were Southern sympathizers. In his narrative, Richardson rendered grateful tribute to the colored people who gave him assistance, not forgetting the generous-minded Confederates, but probably a question of taste led him to keep silent regarding Free Masons. It is a fact, nonetheless, that his membership of that order saved his life in more than one instance.

Elijah Simerley lived at Doe River Cove (now Hampton), Carter County, East Tenn. His family consisted of his wife—living in 1907—and thirteen children. His funeral in 1901 was attended by five of his sons and five of his daughters. His wife was Mary Hampton, a distant relative of General Wade Hampton.

Simerley was a man of marked ability and many noble qualities, which endeared him to his friends. He owned a large tract of land, a comfortable home, and was in good circumstances at the breaking out of the war, though impoverished at its close. His business was that of dealing in cattle, and he often purchased and sold droves of hundreds of the animals. From a rich iron ore mine on his property he manufactured large quantities of hammered iron, which during those trying days passed as currency in that section.

As evidence of the character of Simerley, it may be said that he was a member of the State Senate before the outbreak of war, he served as high sheriff of Carter County, was collector of United States revenue during the Presidency of Andrew Johnson, and he secured the charter for the first railway (The East Tennessee and West North Carolina) through the mountains from Johnson City to Cranberry, N. C., and was its first president.

Simerley was a pronounced Union man from the beginning. He was a well-known Free Mason and was one of those who helped Albert D. Richardson and other brethren to escape when they were shut in by peril on every hand. It would make a story of surpassing interest, if we were at liberty to tell some of the numerous incidents, but we must confine ourselves to two only, in each of which Simerley figured.

Colonel Robert E. Love was a member of the same Masonic lodge with Simerley, and was the leader of the East Tennessee Bar. He lived on his fine farm about eight miles from the home of Simerley, and the two were warm friends. Colonel Love was a strong secessionist and gave his fine talents to the advancement of the cause that was so dear to his heart. Nonetheless, on two different occasions, he saved the life of Simerley.

The first instance was when the Federal commander, Colonel Kirk, entered East Tennessee from North Carolina, with his regiment. A few days before, Simerley had bought several hundred cattle from Colonel Love. Colonel Kirk's command was in great need of food and Simerley turned the beeves over to the Federal officer. Soon thereafter, Colonel Kirk was compelled to withdraw from the section, and Carter County was taken possession of by the Confederates.

The transaction between the colonel and Simerley was known to everybody and placed the latter in a perilous situation. When the Union troops were out of the way, a council of the leading secessionists was held to decide what should be done with Simerley. Colonel Love was a member of this council, which was really a court to determine the degree of punishment to be dealt out to the accused. In those times, about the only degree of punishment in fashion was that of death: nothing less counted.

When the other members of the council had expressed their sentiments in favor of shooting or hanging Simerley, Colonel Love, with the pleasing smile and winning manner so familiar to those who remember him, said:

"There can be no question of what ought to be done with a man who gives aid and comfort to the enemy. Tennessee is a member of the Southern Confederacy, and all who are not the friends of the Confederacy are its enemies. But you have made one mistake, gentlemen."

His friends looked wonderingly at the lawyer.

"Those cattle taken away by Colonel Kirk were mine; I can assure you that it is no small loss I have suffered, but it is not as great as hundreds of other good men have undergone. It would be hardly fair to punish Simerley because the Federal invaders stole a lot of *my* cattle."

This put another face on the matter. It is well that the other members of the court accepted the word of Colonel Love unquestioningly, and made no further investigation, but the fib told by Colonel Love saved the life of the daring Unionist of the time.

In my "Ten Years Later", I said that Wilkins, who escaped death through the friendship of the Confederate Secretary of War, was not a bridge burner. He assured me that this statement was the strict truth, and there was no reason why he should try to deceive me. In the case of Simerley, however, he, like Dan Ellis, was one of the most active bridge burners in East Tennessee. He had a hand in the destruction of several of the valuable structures. This so crippled the transfer of troops and supplies for the Confederacy, that it is easy to understand why the authorities showed scant mercy to the men who were proved guilty of the incendiarism. Simerley knew he would receive short shrift if the officers could lay hands on him.

It was necessary therefore, to be always on the alert. Many an hour did the present Mrs. Badgley, who was then a young girl, sit on top of the high gatepost, shading her eyes with one hand, while her keen eyes peered up and down the highway in quest of that which she dreaded to see. Alas, she or her little brothers or sisters did catch sight of those forms more than once, and were quick to give the alarm. Instantly the father skurried to the mountains, whither it would have taken a bloodhound to trail him. He returned only when the coast was clear. Night after night, he dared not sleep under his own roof. As it was, some of the men who worked with him grew careless and their lives paid the forfeit.

Carter's Depot was near the bridge across the Watauga River, and was the site of a large camp of Confederates. Elizabethton was nearly half way between the camp and the home of Simerley, the whole distance being over twelve miles. From Elizabethton to Doe River Cove, where Simerley lived, was seven miles by what was known as the Gap Creek road.

One day Colonel Love saw four Confederate cavalrymen and a captain gallop into Elizabethton. Love approached the officer.

"May I ask, captain, your business in this little town?"

"Certainly, colonel," replied the officer, returning the salute. He knew Love well, as did every one in that section; "I have orders to bring in 'Lige Simerley dead or alive, and I'm going to do it."

"But, captain, where is your force?"

"There," replied the officer with a smile, indicating his four cavalrymen.

"For God's Sake, 'Lige, Flee to the Mountains!"   227

Colonel Love recoiled a step and threw up his hands.

"Great heavens! Do you expect to capture 'Lige Simerley with only four troopers?"

"Why not?"

The colonel pointed up the Gap, which was deeply wooded on both sides.

"You see those woods; they are full of bushwhackers; if you venture to ride through the Gap every saddle will be emptied within a mile of where we are standing; it is inexcusable folly for you to make the attempt."

The captain was impressed. He knew Colonel Love too well to doubt his words. He hesitated.

"I have my orders, colonel."

"But given under a misapprehension."

"What do you advise me to do?"

"Go back to camp at once and report what I have said to you."

"How large a company should I take with me?"

"Twenty men at least; see that they are well mounted; of course they will be armed; and make up your mind to have a sharp fight before you make 'Lige Simerley a prisoner."

"Thank you, colonel," replied the captain, with a military salute, as he turned and gave the order to his men to ride back to camp.

Colonel Love watched the galloping troopers until they passed out of sight at the lower end of the town. Then he looked around and saw Larry O'Brien on the opposite side of the street, chatting with some friends. He had ridden into town a short time before, and was exchanging gossip with a number of his acquaintances.

No old resident of that section can ever forget Larry O'Brien. Despite his name, he was a native Tennessean, short of stature, brawny, with a full beard and the jolliest wag of the county. He was a bachelor in middle life, and had the reputation of having kissed more young women in the neighborhood than any other man. In that respect, he ran a close second to General Sherman. At the picnics, as everywhere else, he was a favorite, for there was no resisting his good nature and big heart. Old, middle-aged men and women, and even the children were fond of him. After the close of the war, Larry was employed for a number of years in the folding room of the House of Representatives in Washington. Let it be remembered, too, that Larry was a Free Mason.

Colonel Love took out his notebook and hastily wrote in pencil:

"For God's sake, 'Lige, flee to the mountains. They are after you."

Crossing the street, the colonel nodded to Larry, and motioned him to draw aside. When they were beyond earshot of the other members of the group, the colonel handed the folded slip of paper to Larry.

"The captain who has just ridden away with his squad has orders to bring in 'Lige Simerley dead or alive. Will you carry this note to him?"

"If my horse doesn't drop dead I'll put it into his hands sooner than any other mortal can do it."

"You can add the few words of explanation necessary; you haven't a minute to spare."

Larry shoved the bit of paper into his trousers' pocket, strode to where his horse was tied to a hitching post, hastily unfastened him and swung into the saddle. It was seven miles by the Gap road to the home of Simerley and five miles to the Confederate camp. The cavalry were certain to be well mounted, for they knew the need of haste. Colonel Love watched Larry as he rode at an easy pace out of town.

"Ride, Larry, ride, for a life is at stake!"

The shrewd fellow did not wish to draw attention to himself, for it might awaken suspicion and make things unpleasant for Colonel Love. When he had disappeared, the colonel sauntered away as if the matter was of little or no importance. If his act of friendship became known to the Confederate authorities, even his prominent place in the community and his well-known Southern sympathies might not save him from the gravest consequences. His only anxiety, however, was lest the faithful messenger should not reach the home of Elijah Simerley in time to save his life.

Note the situation: Colonel Love, a Free Mason and a Secessionist, was sending a message to another Mason, an obnoxious Unionist and bridge burner, who could expect no mercy at the hands of the Confederate authorities; and the bearer of the warning was a Free Mason.

As soon as Larry O'Brien had shaken himself free of the little town, he loosened the reins of his nag, struck his flanks with his spurs and spoke sharply. The beast instantly changed from a canter to a dead run. With neck outstretched and with tail streaming in the wind created by his own motion, he ran at the very highest speed of which he was capable. Although Colonel Love had said that the wooded mountains that rose on either hand were swarming with bushwhackers, he exaggerated the truth, yet beyond question a number of those undesirable persons were lurking there. They might take a shot at the flying horseman and tumble him from his saddle, but Larry felt slight misgivings on that score. He was too well known to fear the Unionists, and they were the only ones that were likely to note his terrific dash over the Gap road.

No, Larry's only dread was that of failure to reach the Simerley home in time. It would seem that this ought to be easy, since he had but seven miles to travel, while the troopers were obliged to go much farther—that is, in riding to their camp and in returning. But suppose Larry's nag should cast a shoe and go lame; the highway was rough, and traveling at such a tremendous pace the animal was liable to suffer some injury that would compel him to withdraw from the task. If so, Larry would continue the desperate run on foot, but with slight hope of distancing his pursuers, who would be thundering on his heels.

I do not know how long Larry took to cover the seven miles between Elizabethton and the home of Elijah Simerley, nor is it important to know. Suffice it to say he didn't loiter on the way; and of all the hard rides, and they were many, taken by the messenger, that seven miles were the hardest. Doubtless some of the prowling bushwhackers peered through the foliage at the hurrying horseman, and made ready to shoot him from his saddle, but if so, that broad, dumpy figure in slouch hat, with head bent forward and loose rein, while he urged his steed to do his best, was recognized, and no deadly bullet whistled from the coverts on either side of the road.

"It's Larry O'Brien; God go with him," must have been the thought of all such persons.

They were always on the lookout at the Simerley home, and the approaching horseman was seen riding like mad, and evidently bringing momentous news. As he reined up his panting animal, whose flanks were heaving, and who was covered with foamy sweat, Simerley himself, his wife and several children were awaiting him. O'Brien was identified while some distance away, and received the cordial welcome that awaited him at almost every home for scores of miles around.

"What is it, Larry?" asked Simerley, hurrying to the side of the messenger.

"For God's Sake, 'Lige, Flee to the Mountains!"

O'Brien handed him the slip of paper, which Simerley opened and quickly read. He turned to his anxious family and repeated its words. Larry added a few sentences that told everything. "Simerley thanked him and invited him to dismount. He shook his head.

"It won't do, 'Lige, thank you, and I daren't go back by the Gap road; I should meet the troopers that are after you; I must take a roundabout course to Elizabethton; you mustn't wait, Simerley."

"I don't intend to wait," was the reply; "I know what that warning from Colonel Love means."

Simerley bade his family a hasty good-by and plunged into the wooded slope at the rear of his home. It seemed to the family as if he and O'Brien had been gone only a few minutes when the cavalrymen arrived. They had certainly ridden hard and the captain was resolute to obey his orders to take back Elijah Simerley dead or alive.

The declaration of the wife that the head was not at home carried no weight with them. They dismounted and searched the house from attic to cellar, and examined all the outbuildings so minutely that a cat could not have escaped their vigilance.

But they didn't find Elijah Simerley.

XIX

THE ABDUCTION OF WILLIAM MORGAN

IN 1821 William Morgan was a brewer, living in York, Upper Canada. Unsuccessful in that business, he removed to Rochester, N. Y., and wrought at his trade of stonemason. He was a ne'er-do-well, addicted to tippling, spent most of his time in saloons, and was a man whose word few would accept. Two years later, he changed his home to Batavia, Genesee County, in the same State.

It is doubtful whether Morgan was ever made a Free Mason, though he may have received the degrees in Canada. He succeeded, however, in convincing a number of the brethren that he had passed through the "Blue Lodge," and was allowed to enter the one at Batavia. He made oath that he had been regularly entered, passed and raised, and he was made a Royal Arch Mason at LeRoy, N. Y., on the last day of May 1823. A movement was set on foot to establish a Royal Arch Chapter at Batavia, and Morgan signed the petition for that purpose, in 1826. His character was so well known that most of the other signers objected to the appearance of his name on the petition, and a new one was substituted, from which it was omitted. This curt snub not only angered Morgan, but also implanted in his sodden brain the resolve to expose the secrets of the order, by which he was confident that he and his associates would

The Abduction of William Morgan

gain a great fortune.

He secured an ally in David C. Miller, editor of the *Republican Advocate*, a weekly paper published at Batavia. It is said that this man had received the first degree in Masonry, but being found unworthy, was never advanced further. He was involved in debt, and, like Morgan, believed that the treachery would make all concerned independently rich. The editor did not shrink from publicly announcing his purpose.

It was right here that the Masons made a blunder, which, in the language of the French, was worse than a crime. They should have paid no attention to the treachery, and the publication, whatever it might have been, would have fallen flat and attracted little or no notice. Strong arguments were made to Morgan to abandon his scheme, and he said he was willing to do so, but Miller pushed the publication as fast as he could. Several hotheaded Masons determined to get the manuscript. Miller's office was set on fire in September, but the flames were extinguished before much damage was done. A reward of $100 was offered for the arrest and conviction of the incendiary, but the secret was well guarded. There were not wanting those who believed that Miller had set fire to the building as a shrewd means of advertising.

Morgan owed a sum of money to a hotelkeeper at Canandaigua, and he was arrested for the debt and taken thither. He was acquitted, but arrested again on a similar charge, confessed judgment and was lodged in jail. Miller was also arrested, but he eluded the officer and fled to his home. The wife of Morgan hurried to Canandaigua to the aid of her husband, but learning that the debt had been paid, returned, having been told that her husband would speedily join her.

When several days passed without his appearance, she became alarmed and sent a friend to learn what it meant. He came back with word that the debt had been settled and Morgan released, but he had hardly left jail when he was seized by Loton Lawson and another person and hustled down the street. He resisted violently and shouted "Murder!" Nicholas G. Chesebro and Edward Sawyer, who with Lawson were members of the posse that had brought Morgan from home, were spectators who refused to help the prisoner. They followed the others, and were in turn followed by a carriage, which soon came back and was driven toward Rochester. It was empty when it went away, but contained several persons on its return. The messenger of Mrs. Morgan reported that the carriage reached Rochester at daybreak and was driven three miles beyond. At that point, the party left it, and the vehicle returned. The driver swore that all the men were strangers to him and that he saw no violence.

Here another point is reached upon which the truth will never be clearly known. Many have contended that no personal harm was intended, but that the purpose of the abductors was to compel Morgan to abandon his scheme and to leave the country, the promise being made to him that he would be provided with a liberal sum of money. It is said further that he agreed to do as proposed, that he received the money and buried himself out of sight of all his former acquaintances. Reports came from time to time that he had been recognized in South America, in Turkey, in the wilds of Canada, and in other parts of the world, but all these reports were baseless. The miserable fellow had disappeared as utterly as if the ground had opened and swallowed him from human sight.

The high-handed outrage started a wave of excitement which swept over the entire country. The abduction of

Morgan was without palliation, even if no personal harm was meditated against him. The guilty parties should have been punished with the utmost rigor of the law. Among the thousands who hotly condemned the crime were leading Free Masons, who gave their help to running down the criminals.

As is invariably the case, the innocent had to suffer for the guilty. Public meetings were held in Batavia and elsewhere, in which the fraternity was denounced in the fiercest terms. Only those who lived in the Border States at the outbreak of the Civil War can form any idea of the irrestrainable rage that was stirred to its depths. Although Governor De Witt Clinton was a prominent Mason, he issued a proclamation, October 7, 1826, calling upon all officers and ministers of justice to use the most efficient measures to arrest the offenders and to bring them to justice. Shortly after, he followed with a second proclamation, offering a reward for the arrest and conviction of the guilty persons. In the following March, a third proclamation promised $1000 to any one who, "as accomplice or co-operator, shall make a full discovery of the offender or offenders."

The investigations thus set on foot showed that when the men left the carriage beyond Rochester on the fateful morning, they entered another vehicle and went westward by the way of Clarkson, Gaines, Lewiston and thus to Fort Niagara, where they arrived the following morning. On a portion of the journey, Sheriff Bruce of the county was with them. At Fort Niagara, the four men dismissed the carriage and made their way to the fort, which was near at hand. Beyond this, it was impossible to trace the parties farther. With them disappeared William Morgan.

In arriving at a clear judgment of the truth concerning this lamentable affair, it must be borne in mind that naturally both parties to the controversy were biased. The accusers of the fraternity were impulsive, hot headed, intemperate and unjust, inasmuch as they laid the blame at the door of the order, when in truth the vast majority condemned the crime as warmly as their opponents. On the other hand, the Free Masons labored to make the case as favorable as they could. By that is meant that they insisted that no personal harm was intended or ever perpetrated against the man, who willingly agreed to guide himself in accordance with the wishes of his abductors.

The father of the writer was a neighbor of Morgan, knew the persons accused and gave it as his belief, expressed many years after, that Morgan was placed in a boat or flung overboard and sent over Niagara Falls.

The direct outcome of the disappearance of Morgan was the formation of the anti-Masonic party, whose leaders were William H. Seward, Millard Fillmore, William Wirt (attorney-general under Monroe), John Quincy Adams and that adroit politician, Thurlow Weed. During the four years ending in 1831, some one or other connected with the abduction was in jail, and suits were prosecuted for a long time. Sheriff Bruce was removed from office by Governor Clinton. He also suffered imprisonment for a year and a half. The sheriff always contended that Morgan voluntarily accompanied the parties who had him in charge. Loton Lawson was sentenced for a term of two years, Nicholas G. Chesebro for one year and Edward Sawyer for one month. The natural question that presents itself at this point is that if Morgan was alive, why was he not traced—as he certainly could have been—and restored to his friends? In truth, he was and had been dead for a good while.

The resentment against Free Masonry flamed into a fire that threatened to sweep everything before it. In many places, clergymen were not allowed to preach unless they repudiated and denounced Masonry, and Masonic meetings were prevented by force of arms. In several of the States, the Grand Lodges felt it advisable to suspend their meetings for years. In Vermont, every lodge stopped work. It is the pride of my own lodge (Trenton, No. 5) that it did not miss a single communication throughout all those tempestuous years, being the only one in New Jersey that thus braved the storm. The old lodge room was on the bank of the Delaware, and in order to reach it the members stole through alleys and along the shore until it was safe to dodge to the door where the trembling Tyler admitted them. Many of those who were warmly attached to the order, after passing temperate resolutions, counselled a yielding for the time to the persecution, a closing of their work and the surrender of their charters. This was extensively done. As evidence of the staggering blow to Masonry, it may be stated that although the Grand Lodge of Maine met annually from 1834 to 1843, it once had not a single representative from any lodge, and only twice during that period did it have representatives from more than four lodges. The lodges in New Jersey were reduced from thirty-three to six in number.

The cruellest charge was that Governor Clinton committed suicide in 1828 because of his remorse for sanctioning the death of Morgan. Only a few months before his death he had declared that Free Masonry was no more responsible for the acts of unworthy members than any other institution or association.

No occurrence, however tragic, is safe from misuse by the politicians. More than a hundred anti-Masonic newspapers sprang into existence, whose venomous opposition was beyond description. Chief among these was the *Albany Evening Journal,* under the control of Thurlow Weed, a representative of Monroe County in the Legislature. No language was too inflammatory for this and the other papers.

On October 7, 1827, the body of a drowned man was found on the beach of Lake Ontario, forty miles from Niagara. It was so decomposed that recognition was impossible, and the coroner's jury, having rendered a verdict of accidental death, the remains were buried. The golden opportunity was not lost by Weed. He and several men, including David C. Miller, had the grave reopened. At the second inquest, Mrs. Morgan and other witnesses identified the body of her husband. The fact that the clothing was such as Morgan had never been known to wear, and that he had been missing for more than a year, and that no perceptible physical resemblance could be noted, did not prevent the official declaration that the remains were those of William Morgan. It was on this occasion that Thurlow Weed is said to have replied to the absurdity of the whole business by the grim declaration, "It's a good enough Morgan till after election."

The evidence that the remains were not those of the Morgan became so clear that a third inquest was held in the latter part of 1827. It was then established beyond question that the body was that of Timothy Monro, whose boat had been upset while crossing the river some weeks previous.

Thurlow Weed, in a letter published September 9, 1882, said that John Whitney, while at his house in 1831, confessed that he and four others, whom he named, told Morgan, who was confined in a magazine at Fort Niagara, that arrangements had been made for sending him to Canada, where his family would soon follow him; that Morgan consented and walked with the party to a boat, which was rowed to the mouth of the river, where a rope was wound around Morgan's body, to each end of which a sinker was attached, and he was then thrown overboard. Weed said he could not in honor reveal, a secret thus imparted to him. Twenty-nine years later, when Weed was attending a National Republican Convention in Chicago, where John Whitney lived, the latter called upon him with the request that he would write out what he had told him in 1831, have it witnessed, sealed up and published after his death. Weed promised to do so, but in the hurry and excitement of the convention, which nominated Abraham Lincoln for the Presidency, he overlooked the matter. In 1861, Weed while in London wrote to Whitney, asking him to get Alexander B. Williams of Chicago to perform the duty, which Weed had so unpardonably neglected. Whitney died just before the letter reached Chicago.

Such was Weed's statement, but the fact remains that Whitney did not die until eight years after the date given by Weed, and witnesses came forward who declared that they heard Whitney angrily protest to Weed against his persistent falsehoods about him.

To return, the anti-Masonic party grew rapidly in numbers. At first, it was confined to western New York, where, in 1828, its candidate for Governor received 33,345 votes, not enough, however, to elect him. In the following year, in the State election, the anti-Masons carried fifteen counties and polled 67,000 votes. In 1830 and 1832, Francis Granger, the nominee of the anti-Masonic party, received a large vote, but not sufficient in either case to bring him success. In the State of New York, the vote of 33,345 in 1828 rose to 156,672 in 1832. In the last-named year, the anti-Masonic party entered the Presidential field, nominating William Wirt of Maryland and Amos Ellmaker of Pennsylvania respectively for President and Vice-President. This ticket received all the electoral votes of Vermont. It should be noted, too, that in 1836 Francis Granger was nominated on the ticket with General William Henry Harrison. After that, the opposition to Free Masonry died out almost as rapidly as it had arisen, and the order was never more flourishing than it is to-day.

Those who recall the devious ways of Thurlow Weed will hardly believe the statement he made about John Whitney, in view of the inaccuracy that his London letter of 1861 did not reach Chicago until after the death of Whitney, who lived until 1869. Whitney did leave a statement, which was not to be published until after his death, and not then unless a new attack should be made upon Free Masonry.

Whitney declared that the plan from inception to completion had in view nothing more than a deportation of Morgan, by friendly agreement between the parties, either to Canada or some other country. Ample means were provided for the support of Morgan's family, and for giving him a fair start in life. Morgan agreed to everything proposed. He was to destroy all MSS., gradually cease drinking, refuse to meet his former partners, and to go to Canada, if necessary, on an hour's notice. When he reached his appointed place, he was to be paid $500 upon his written pledge not to return to the States. His family was to be sent to him with as little delay as possible.

It will be recalled that Morgan was released from jail upon the payment of his debt. This was part of the prearranged plan, and Morgan understood it all. Unfortunately, he had obtained liquor, which always made him violent, and he fiercely resisted, until he realized his mistake, when he yielded and got into the carriage as quietly as did the other members of the party. Whitney accompanied the coach from Canandaigua. The sheriff joined the party at Wright's Corners and they drove to Youngstown, where they called upon Colonel William King, an officer of the War of 1812.

The Abduction of William Morgan

From this point, we quote:

"King and Bruce got into the carriage together and had a long conversation with Morgan. The whole transaction was gone over and Morgan gave his assent and concurrence therewith.

"On arriving near the fort, the driver (not a Mason) was dismissed and the coach sent back. The ferryboat was ready and the party went immediately on board. It was rowed by Elisha Adams nearly opposite the fort and about a mile from the Canadian village of Niagara. Leaving Morgan in the boat, three of the party went to the village and met a committee of two Canadian Masons as agreed.

"No official inquiry has ever brought out the names of these, and I shall ever be silent concerning them. We came back to the boat, the Canadian brethren bringing a lantern. Bruce called Morgan up the bank, out of the boat, and the party sat down together on the grass. Now Colonel King required of Morgan the most explicit consent to the movements that had brought him there. By the aid of questions from the whole party, Morgan admitted as follows:

"'(1) That he had contracted with Miller and others to write an exposition of Masonry, for which he was to receive a compensation.

"'(2) That he had never been made a Mason in any lodge, but had received the Royal Arch degree in a regular manner.

"'(3) That Miller and the other partners had utterly failed to fulfil the terms of the contract with him.

"'(4) That Whitney had paid him $50, as agreed, and he had agreed to destroy the written and printed work as far as possible and furnish no more, and that before leaving Batavia he had done what he promised in that way.

"'(5) That it was impossible now for Miller to continue

The "illustrations" as he [Morgan] had written them. If he published any book, it would have to be made from some other person's materials.

"'(6) That he had been treated by Chesebro, Whitney, Bruce, and all of them with perfect kindness on the journey.

"'(7) That he was willing and anxious to be separated from Miller and from all idea of a Masonic *exposé;* wished to go into the interior of Canada and settle down as a British citizen; wished to have his family sent to him as soon as possible; expected $500 when he reached the place, as agreed upon; expected more money from year to year, to help him, if necessary.

"'(8) Finally he expressed his sorrow for the uproar his proceedings had made, sorrow for the shame and mortification of his friends, and had "no idea that David C. Miller was such a d—scoundrel as he had turned out to be."'

"We had ascertained at the village that the Canadian brethren would be ready to perform their part and remove Morgan westward by the latter part of that or the first of the succeeding week, but objected so strenuously to having him remain among them in the meantime, that it was agreed that he [Morgan] should be taken to the American side until the Canadians should notify us that they were ready.

"This was explained to Morgan, and he agreed to it. It was then understood that he was to remain in the magazine without attempting to get out until matters were arranged for his removal. The party then rowed back, and Morgan was left in the bomb proof of the magazine.

"The party then left, breakfasted at Youngstown, and went up to Lewiston on the Rochester boat that passed up, with passengers for the Royal Arch installation that occurred there that day. There was quite a company of us there, and the intelligence was freely communicated that Morgan was

The Traitor. "That was the last ever heard of him"

in Fort Niagara, and the greatest satisfaction was expressed at the news that the manuscripts and printed sheets had been destroyed, and that in a few days Morgan would be effectually separated from the company that had led to his ruin. During the day it was reported to us at Lewiston that 'Morgan had gone into theatricals,' and was shouting and alarming the people in the vicinity. Nothing would quiet him except rum, which was given him.

"Lawson, Whitney and a few others remained in the vicinity until Sunday night, when the two Canadian brethren came over, received Morgan, receipted to Whitney for the money [$500] and crossed to the west side of the river.

"They travelled on horseback—three horses in the party; Monday night they rode some thirty miles farther to a point near the present city of Hamilton, where the journey ended. Morgan signed a receipt for the $500. He also signed a declaration of the facts in the case.

"We supposed we could at any time trace him up. We felt that the craft would be the gainer by our labors. We were prepared to send his wife and children to him as agreed. We supposed that that was the end of it.

"What a tremendous blunder we all made! It was scarcely a week until we saw that trouble was before us. It was not a fortnight until Colonel King sent a confidential messenger into Canada to see Morgan and prepare to bring him back.

"But alas! He who had sold his friends at Batavia had also sold us. He had gone. He had left the village within forty-eight hours after the departure of those who had taken him there. He was traced east to a point down the river not far from Port Hope, where he sold his horse and disappeared. He had doubtless got on board a vessel there and sailed out of the country. At any rate, that was the last we ever heard of him."

MASONIC GRAND LODGES IN THE UNITED STATES AND BRITISH AMERICA

(From the *World Almanac*)

Grand Lodges	No. Members, 1907	Grand Secretaries	Grand Lodges	No. Members, 1907	Grand Secretaries
Alabama	18,191	G. A. Beauchamp, Montgomery	Nevada	1,113	C. N. Noteware, Carson
Arizona	1,191	G. J. Roskruge, Tucson	New Brunswick*	2,204	J. Twining Hartt, St. John
Arkansas*	17,480	F. Hempstead, Little Rock	New Hampshire	9,695	F. D. Woodbury, Concord
British Columbia	3,051	R. E. Brett, Columbia	New Jersey	24,973	T. H. R. Redway, Trenton
California	33,769	G. Johnson, San Francisco	New Mexico	1,629	A. A. Keen, Albuquerque
Canada	37,000	Hugh Murray, Hamilton	New York	146,026	E. M. L. Ehlers, New York City
Colorado	11,501	C. H. Jacobson, Denver	North Carolina	15,528	John C. Drewry, Raleigh
Connecticut	20,087	John H. Barlow, Hartford	North Dakota	5,567	F. J. Thompson, Fargo
Delaware	2,772	B. F. Bartram, Wilmington	Nova Scotia	4,715	Thomas Mowbray, Halifax
District of Col	7,726	Arvine W. Johnston, Wash.	Ohio	65,107	J. H. Bromwell, Cincinnati
Florida	6,655	W. P. Webster, Jacksonville	Oklahoma	6,777	J. S. Hunt, Stillwater
Georgia	27,620	W. A. Wolihin, Macon	Oregon	7,689	Jas. F. Robinson, Eugene
Idaho	2,251	Theop. W. Randall, Boise	Pennsylvania	71,249	Wm. A. Sinn, Philadelphia
Illinois	79,712	Isaac Cutter, Coup Point	Prince Ed. Island	635	N. MacKelvie, Summerside
Indiana	45,059	C. W. Prather, Indianapolis	Quebec	5,000	Will. H. Whyte, Montreal
Indian Territory	7,540	J. S. Murrow, Atoka	Rhode Island	6,483	S. P. Williams, Providence
Iowa	36,736	N. R. Parvin, Cedar Rapids	South Carolina	8,688	Jacob T. Barron, Columbia
Kansas	27,167	Albert K. Wilson, Topeka	South Dakota	6,636	G. A. Pettigrew, Flandreau
Kentucky	28,593	H. B. Grant, Louisville	Tennessee	20,579	John B. Garrett, Nashville
Louisiana	9,651	R. Lambert, New Orleans	Texas	39,162	John Watson, Waco
Maine	25,889	Stephen Berry, Portland	Utah	1,270	C. Diehl, Salt Lake City
Manitoba	4,410	James A. Ovas, Winnipeg	Vermont	11,802	H. H. Ross, Burlington
Maryland	11,057	Wm. M. Isaac, Baltimore	Virginia	16,981	G. W. Carrington, Richmond
Massachusetts	50,328	S. D. Nickerson, Boston	Washington	9,880	Horace W. Tyler, Seattle
Michigan	53,795	L. B. Winsor, Reed City	West Virginia	11,006	H. R. Howard, Point Pleasant
Minnesota	20,287	T. Montgomery, St. Paul	Wisconsin	22,118	Wm. W. Perry, Milwaukee
Mississippi	13,252	F. Speed, Vicksburg	Wyoming	1,951	W. L. Kuykendall, Saratoga
Missouri	42,924	J. R. Parson, St. Louis			
Montana	4,227	Cornelius Hedges, Helena	Total	1,188,566	
Nebraska	15,163	Francis E. White, Omaha			

The returns of the Grand Lodges of the United States and British America for 1905-1906 were as follows: Whole number of members, 1,062,425; raised, 81,386; admissions and restorations, 28,155; withdrawals, 22,008; expulsions and suspensions, 659; suspensions for non-payment of dues, 12,760; deaths, 16,123. Gain in membership over preceding year, 58,177. Membership in 1906, 1,129,001; gain over the preceding year of 66,576.
*Report of 1906.

Look for these and other great titles at:
http://www.stoneguildpublishing.com

Book of Ancient and Accepted Scottish Rite by Charles T. McClenachan

The Book of the Holy Graal by A. E. Waite

The Book of the Lodge by George Oliver

The Builders by Joseph Fort Newton

Chymical Marriage of Christian Rosencreutz translated by A. E. Waite

The Doctrine and Literature of the Kabalah by A. E. Waite

Fama Fraternitatis and Confession of the Rosicrucians by A. E. Waite

Freemasonry in the Holy Land by Robert Morris

The Freemason's Manual by Jeremiah How

The Freemason's Monitor by Daniel Sickels

The History of Freemasonry and Concordant Orders

The History of Initiation by George Oliver

Illustrations of the Symbols of Freemasonry by Jacob Ernst

The Kybalion by The Three Initiates

Low Twelve by Edward S. Ellis

The New Masonic Trestleboard by Charles W. Moore

Opinions on Speculative Masonry by James C. Odiorne

The Perfect Ceremonies of Craft Masonry

The Poetry of Freemasonry by Rob Morris

Real History of the Rosicrucians by A. E. Waite

The Symbolism of Freemasonry by Albert G. Mackey

Symbolism of the Three Degrees by Oliver Day Street

Taylor's Monitor by William M. Taylor

Taylor-Hamilton Monitor of Symbolic Masonry by Sam R. Hamilton

Three Hundred Masonic Odes and Poems by Rob Morris

True Masonic Chart or Hieroglyphic Monitor by Jeremy Cross